Affiliate Marketing Mastery: Unleashing Six-Figure Income

Introduction to Affiliate Marketing

1.1 What is Affiliate Marketing?

Affiliate marketing is a popular online business model that allows individuals to earn a commission by promoting other people's products or services. It is a performance-based marketing strategy where affiliates (also known as publishers) earn a commission for driving traffic or generating sales for the merchant (also known as the advertiser).

In simple terms, affiliate marketing works like this: an affiliate promotes a product or service through various marketing channels such as websites, blogs, social media, email marketing, or paid advertising. When a customer clicks on the affiliate's unique tracking link and makes a purchase, the affiliate earns a commission.

Affiliate marketing is a win-win situation for both the affiliate and the merchant. The affiliate earns a commission for each successful referral, while the merchant gains exposure and increases sales without spending a significant amount on traditional advertising.

Affiliate marketing is a versatile business model that can be applied to various industries and niches. It allows individuals to earn passive income by leveraging their online presence and marketing skills. With the right strategies and dedication, affiliate marketing has the potential to generate a six-figure income per month.

To succeed in affiliate marketing, it is essential to understand the key components of the process:

1. **Affiliate**: An individual or entity that promotes products or services through various marketing channels.

2. **Merchant**: The company or individual that owns the product or service being promoted. They provide the affiliate with unique tracking links and handle the order fulfillment process.

3. **Consumer**: The end-user who purchases the product or service through the affiliate's referral link.

4. **Affiliate Network**: An intermediary platform that connects affiliates with merchants. It provides tracking, reporting, and payment services.

5. **Commission**: The percentage or fixed amount that the affiliate earns for each successful referral or sale.

Affiliate marketing offers several benefits that make it an attractive business model:

- **Low Startup Costs**: Unlike traditional businesses, affiliate marketing requires minimal upfront investment. You can get started with as little as a domain name and web hosting.

- **No Product Creation**: As an affiliate, you don't need to create your own products or services. You can focus on promoting existing products and earning a commission.

- **Flexible Work Schedule**: Affiliate marketing allows you to work from anywhere and at any time. You have the freedom to choose your own schedule and work at your own pace.

- **Passive Income Potential**: Once you set up your affiliate marketing campaigns and start driving traffic, you can earn passive income. This means that you can continue earning commissions even when you're not actively promoting.

- **Scalability**: Affiliate marketing offers the potential for exponential growth. As you gain experience and optimize your strategies, you can scale your business by promoting multiple products or expanding into new niches.

- **Diverse Income Streams**: With affiliate marketing, you have the opportunity to promote products from various merchants and earn multiple streams of income.

- **No Customer Support or Inventory Management**: As an affiliate, you don't have to deal with customer support or inventory management. The merchant handles these aspects, allowing you to focus on marketing and driving traffic.

Affiliate marketing is a dynamic and ever-evolving industry. To succeed and earn a six-figure income per month, it is crucial to stay updated with the latest trends, strategies, and techniques. This book will guide you through the entire affiliate marketing process, from choosing profitable niches to driving targeted traffic and optimizing your campaigns for maximum conversions.

1.2 Benefits of Affiliate Marketing

Affiliate marketing is a powerful business model that offers numerous benefits to individuals looking to earn a substantial income online. In this section, we will explore the key advantages of affiliate marketing and why it has become a popular choice for those seeking financial freedom and flexibility.

1. Passive Income Potential

One of the most significant benefits of affiliate marketing is the potential to earn passive income. Unlike traditional employment where you exchange your time for money, affiliate marketing allows you to generate income even while you sleep. Once you have set up your affiliate campaigns and established a steady stream of traffic, you can earn commissions on autopilot. This means that you can continue to earn money from your affiliate links and promotions long after you have completed the initial work.

2. Low Startup Costs

Affiliate marketing is an attractive option for individuals with limited capital because it requires minimal investment to get started. Unlike starting a brick-and-mortar business or developing your own products, affiliate marketing allows you to promote other people's products or services without the need for inventory or upfront costs. With as little as a $100 investment, you can create a website, set up hosting, and begin promoting affiliate offers.

3. No Product Creation or Customer Support

One of the biggest advantages of affiliate marketing is that you don't have to worry about creating your own products or providing customer support. As an affiliate marketer, your primary responsibility is to drive traffic and promote products or services. The product creation, inventory management, and customer support are handled by the merchant or product owner. This allows you to focus on marketing and generating sales, without the added complexities and responsibilities of product development and customer service.

4. Wide Range of Products and Niches

Affiliate marketing offers a vast array of products and niches to choose from. Whether you have a passion for health and wellness, technology, fashion, or any other industry, there are affiliate programs available for almost every niche. This allows you to align your affiliate marketing efforts with your interests and expertise, making the process more enjoyable and fulfilling. Additionally, the wide range of products and niches provides ample opportunities to diversify your income streams and explore different markets.

5. Flexibility and Freedom

Affiliate marketing provides unparalleled flexibility and freedom in terms of work schedule and location. As an affiliate marketer, you have the freedom to work from anywhere in the world as long as you have an internet connection. This means you can work from the comfort of your own home, while traveling, or even while enjoying a coffee at your favorite café. Additionally, affiliate marketing allows you to set your own work hours, giving you the flexibility to work at your own pace and balance your personal and professional life.

Another significant benefit of affiliate marketing is its scalability and growth potential. As you gain experience and refine your marketing strategies, you can scale your affiliate business to reach a larger audience and generate higher commissions. With the right combination of traffic generation techniques, conversion optimization, and strategic partnerships, you can exponentially increase your income and achieve six-figure earnings per month. Additionally, affiliate marketing allows you to expand into new niches and markets, further diversifying your income streams and maximizing your earning potential.

Compared to other business models, affiliate marketing carries minimal risk and offers a high return on investment (ROI). With low startup costs and no need to create your own products, the risk of financial loss is significantly reduced. Additionally, the potential for high commissions and passive income allows you to achieve a substantial ROI on your time and effort. By focusing on effective marketing strategies and building a strong online presence, you can maximize your earnings and minimize the risk associated with traditional business ventures.

In conclusion, affiliate marketing offers a wide range of benefits that make it an attractive option for individuals looking to earn a six-figure income per month. From the potential for passive income and low startup costs to the flexibility and scalability it provides, affiliate marketing allows you to build a profitable online business with minimal risk. By leveraging the power of affiliate marketing, you can unleash your earning potential and achieve financial freedom.

1.3 Understanding the Affiliate Marketing Process

Affiliate marketing is a powerful business model that allows individuals to earn a passive income by promoting other people's products or services. It involves three main parties: the affiliate marketer, the merchant, and the customer. In this section, we will delve into the affiliate marketing process and understand how it works.

The Affiliate Marketer

The affiliate marketer is the driving force behind the entire process. Their role is to promote products or services and earn a commission for every sale or lead generated through their efforts. To become an affiliate marketer, you need to follow these steps:

1. **Choose a niche**: Start by selecting a niche that aligns with your interests, knowledge, and passion. This will make it easier for you to create content and connect with your target audience.

2. **Research affiliate programs**: Once you have chosen a niche, research and identify affiliate programs that offer products or services related to your niche.

Look for programs that provide attractive commission rates, reliable tracking systems, and good support.

3. **Join affiliate programs**: Sign up for the affiliate programs that you have identified. Most programs have a simple registration process that requires basic information about yourself and your website (if you have one).

4. **Promote affiliate products**: After joining the affiliate programs, you will receive unique affiliate links or banners that you can use to promote the products or services. Incorporate these links into your content, such as blog posts, social media posts, or email newsletters.

5. **Drive traffic to your affiliate links**: The success of your affiliate marketing efforts depends on your ability to drive targeted traffic to your affiliate links. Implement various marketing strategies such as search engine optimization (SEO), social media marketing, content marketing, and email marketing to attract potential customers.

6. **Track and analyze your results**: It is crucial to track and analyze the performance of your affiliate marketing campaigns. Use tracking tools and analytics to measure the number of clicks, conversions, and revenue generated. This data will help you optimize your strategies and improve your results.

The Merchant

The merchant is the individual or company that owns the product or service being promoted. They rely on affiliate marketers to promote their offerings and drive sales or leads. Here's how the merchant's role fits into the affiliate marketing process:

1. **Create an affiliate program**: The merchant sets up an affiliate program that outlines the terms and conditions for affiliates. This includes commission rates, payment methods, and promotional guidelines.

2. **Provide marketing materials**: The merchant provides affiliates with marketing materials such as banners, product images, and promotional content. These materials help affiliates effectively promote the products or services.

3. **Track affiliate sales**: The merchant tracks affiliate sales using unique affiliate links or tracking codes. This allows them to accurately attribute sales to specific affiliates and calculate commissions.

4. **Pay affiliate commissions**: Once the affiliate generates a sale or lead, the merchant pays the affiliate a commission based on the agreed-upon terms. Commissions can be a percentage of the sale value or a fixed amount per lead.

The customer is the final piece of the affiliate marketing process. They are the individuals who purchase the products or services being promoted by the affiliate marketer. Here's how the customer's role fits into the process:

1. **Discover the affiliate's content**: Customers come across the affiliate marketer's content through various channels such as search engines, social media platforms, or email newsletters.

2. **Click on the affiliate link**: When customers find the content valuable and relevant, they click on the affiliate link provided by the affiliate marketer. This link redirects them to the merchant's website.

3. **Make a purchase or complete an action**: Once on the merchant's website, the customer may make a purchase or complete a desired action, such as signing up for a newsletter or filling out a form. This action is tracked by the merchant's affiliate tracking system.

4. **Enjoy the product or service**: After completing the desired action, the customer receives the product or service they purchased and enjoys its benefits.

By understanding the affiliate marketing process and the roles of each party involved, you can effectively navigate the world of affiliate marketing and start earning a passive income. Remember, success in affiliate marketing requires dedication, consistency, and continuous learning.

1.4 Setting Realistic Income Goals

Setting realistic income goals is an essential step in your affiliate marketing journey. While it is possible to earn a six-figure income per month through affiliate marketing, it is important to understand that achieving such results requires time, effort, and a strategic approach. In this section, we will discuss how to set realistic income goals and the factors that can influence your earning potential.

Understanding the Potential of Affiliate Marketing

Affiliate marketing has gained immense popularity in recent years due to its potential to generate passive income. It is a performance-based marketing model where affiliates promote products or services and earn a commission for each sale or action made through their referral. The income potential in affiliate marketing is virtually limitless, as it allows you to earn a percentage of the revenue generated by the products or services you promote.

However, it is crucial to approach affiliate marketing with a realistic mindset. While success stories of affiliates earning six-figure incomes per month exist, they are the result of years of hard work, dedication, and strategic planning. It is important to set achievable goals based on your current resources, skills, and experience.

Several factors can influence your income potential in affiliate marketing. Understanding these factors will help you set realistic goals and develop a strategy to achieve them.

1. **Niche Selection:** The niche you choose plays a significant role in determining your income potential. Some niches are more profitable than others, and it is important to research and select a niche that has a high demand for products or services. Choosing a niche that aligns with your interests and expertise can also contribute to your success.

2. **Product Selection:** The products or services you choose to promote can impact your income potential. It is essential to select products that are in high demand, have a good reputation, and offer attractive commission rates. Additionally, promoting products that align with your target audience's needs and preferences can increase your chances of generating sales.

3. **Target Audience:** Understanding your target audience is crucial for affiliate marketing success. Identifying their needs, preferences, and pain points will help you tailor your marketing efforts to resonate with them. The size and purchasing power of your target audience can also influence your income potential.

4. **Marketing Strategies:** The marketing strategies you employ can significantly impact your income potential. Effective strategies such as search engine optimization (SEO), content marketing, social media marketing, and email marketing can drive targeted traffic to your website and increase your chances of generating sales. It is important to invest time and effort in learning and implementing these strategies effectively.

5. **Conversion Rate:** Your conversion rate, which is the percentage of website visitors who take the desired action (e.g., make a purchase), is a critical factor in determining your income potential. Improving your conversion rate through persuasive content, compelling calls-to-action, and user-friendly website design can significantly impact your earnings.

6. **Competition:** The level of competition in your niche can affect your income potential. Highly competitive niches may require more effort and resources to stand out and generate sales. It is important to evaluate the competition and develop a unique selling proposition to differentiate yourself from others.

Setting Realistic Income Goals

When setting income goals for your affiliate marketing business, it is important to be realistic and consider the factors mentioned above. Here are some steps to help you set achievable income goals:

1. **Assess Your Current Situation:** Evaluate your current resources, skills, and experience in affiliate marketing. Consider the time you can dedicate to your business, your budget, and your knowledge of marketing strategies. This assessment will help you set goals that are attainable within your current circumstances.

2. **Research Income Potential:** Research the income potential in your chosen niche by analyzing successful affiliates in the industry. Look for case studies, success stories, and income reports to get an idea of what is achievable. However, keep in mind that everyone's journey is unique, and your results may vary.

3. **Break Down Your Goals:** Break down your income goals into smaller, achievable milestones. For example, if your ultimate goal is to earn a six-figure income per month, start by setting smaller monthly income targets and gradually work your way up. This approach allows you to track your progress and make adjustments along the way.

4. **Track and Analyze Performance:** Implement tracking systems to monitor your affiliate marketing performance. Analyze key performance indicators (KPIs) such as website traffic, conversion rate, and revenue generated. This data will help you identify areas for improvement and make informed decisions to optimize your income potential.

5. **Continuously Learn and Adapt:** Affiliate marketing is a dynamic field, and staying up-to-date with industry trends and best practices is crucial for long-term success. Invest time in learning new marketing strategies, staying informed about changes in your niche, and adapting your approach accordingly.

Remember, affiliate marketing is not a get-rich-quick scheme. It requires consistent effort, patience, and a long-term perspective. By setting realistic income goals and implementing effective strategies, you can gradually build a successful affiliate marketing business and work towards earning a six-figure income per month.

Choosing Profitable Affiliate Niches

2.1 Researching Profitable Niches

In order to earn a six-figure income per month through affiliate marketing, it is crucial to choose profitable niches. A niche refers to a specific segment of a market that caters to a particular group of people with specific needs or interests. By selecting the right niche, you can target a specific audience and increase your chances of generating high commissions.

Researching profitable niches is the first step towards building a successful affiliate marketing business. This process involves identifying niches that have a high demand for products or services and a relatively low level of competition. Here are some strategies to help you research profitable niches:

1. Identify Your Interests and Passions

Start by brainstorming a list of topics that you are genuinely interested in or passionate about. This could be anything from fitness and health to personal finance or travel. By choosing a niche that aligns with your interests, you will be more motivated to create valuable content and engage with your audience.

2. Conduct Market Research

Once you have identified a few potential niches, it's time to conduct market research to evaluate their profitability. Start by using keyword research tools like Google Keyword Planner or SEMrush to identify the search volume and competition level for relevant keywords within your chosen niches. Look for keywords with a high search volume and low competition as these indicate potential profitable niches.

3. Analyze Affiliate Programs

Next, research and analyze the affiliate programs available within your chosen niches. Look for programs that offer high commission rates, reliable tracking systems, and a wide range of products or services that align with your niche. Consider joining affiliate networks like Amazon Associates, ClickBank, or Commission Junction to gain access to a variety of affiliate programs.

4. Evaluate Profit Potential

To determine the profit potential of a niche, consider factors such as the average commission rate, the average order value, and the conversion rate of the affiliate programs within that niche. Calculate the potential earnings by multiplying the average commission rate by the average order value and the conversion rate. This will give you an estimate of the potential income you can generate from promoting products or services within that niche.

5. Assess Market Demand

Evaluate the demand for products or services within your chosen niches. Look for trends, market growth, and consumer behavior to determine if there is a sustainable demand for the niche. Consider using tools like Google Trends or social media platforms to gauge the popularity and interest in your chosen niche.

6. Study the Competition

Analyze the competition within your chosen niches to understand the level of competition you will face. Look for established websites, blogs, or influencers that are already targeting the same audience. Assess their content, marketing strategies, and audience engagement to identify gaps or opportunities that you can leverage.

7. Consider Evergreen Niches

Evergreen niches are those that have a consistent demand and are not subject to seasonal or temporary trends. Examples of evergreen niches include health and wellness, personal finance, and self-improvement. Choosing an evergreen niche can provide long-term stability and consistent income potential.

8. Test and Refine

Once you have identified a potential profitable niche, it's important to test and refine your strategies. Create a website or blog focused on your chosen niche and start producing valuable content. Monitor your website traffic, engagement metrics, and affiliate earnings to assess the effectiveness of your niche selection and make necessary adjustments.

Remember, choosing a profitable niche is just the first step towards earning a six-figure income per month through affiliate marketing. It requires consistent effort, dedication, and continuous learning to build a successful affiliate marketing business.

2.2 Identifying Target Audiences

In order to succeed in affiliate marketing and earn a six-figure income per month, it is crucial to identify and understand your target audience. Your target audience consists of the specific group of people who are most likely to be interested in the products or services you are promoting as an affiliate marketer. By identifying and targeting the right audience, you can effectively tailor your marketing efforts and increase your chances of generating high-converting traffic and sales.

Here are some steps to help you identify your target audience:

1. Research Your Niche

Before you can identify your target audience, you need to have a clear understanding of your niche. Research your niche thoroughly to gain insights into the products or services you will be promoting. This includes understanding the pain points, desires, and needs of your potential customers within that niche.

2. Define Your Ideal Customer

Once you have a good understanding of your niche, it's time to define your ideal customer. Think about the characteristics, demographics, and psychographics of the people who would be most interested in your affiliate products. Consider factors such as age, gender, location, interests, hobbies, and purchasing behavior. This will help you create a detailed profile of your target audience.

3. Conduct Market Research

Market research is essential for identifying your target audience. Use various research methods such as surveys, interviews, and online tools to gather data and insights about your potential customers. Look for patterns and trends in their behavior, preferences, and needs. This information will help you refine your target audience and create more effective marketing strategies.

4. Analyze Competitors

Analyzing your competitors can provide valuable insights into their target audience. Look at the affiliate marketers who are successful in your niche and study their strategies. Identify the types of customers they are targeting and the marketing channels they are using. This analysis will help you understand the gaps in the market and find unique ways to reach your target audience.

5. Utilize Social Media

Social media platforms are powerful tools for identifying and reaching your target audience. Use platforms like Facebook, Instagram, Twitter, and LinkedIn to search for groups, communities, and pages related to your niche. Engage with these communities and observe the discussions and interests of their members. This will give you a better understanding of your target audience's preferences and needs.

6. Use Analytics Tools

Leverage analytics tools to gather data about your website visitors and their behavior. Tools like Google Analytics can provide valuable insights into the demographics, interests, and browsing habits of your audience. Analyzing this data will help you refine your target audience and optimize your marketing strategies accordingly.

7. Test and Refine

Identifying your target audience is an ongoing process. As you implement your marketing strategies, continuously test and refine your approach. Monitor the performance of your campaigns and analyze the data to identify any gaps or areas for improvement. This iterative process will help you better understand your target audience and optimize your efforts for maximum results.

Remember, identifying your target audience is crucial for the success of your affiliate marketing business. By understanding the needs and preferences of your audience, you can create targeted and compelling content that resonates with them. This will ultimately lead to higher conversions and increased affiliate income.

Investing $100 in your affiliate marketing business can be a great starting point, but it's important to note that success in affiliate marketing is not solely dependent on the amount of money you invest. It requires dedication, hard work, and a strategic approach. While $100 can be used for various purposes such as website hosting, domain registration, or paid advertising, it's essential to focus on the quality of your efforts rather than the quantity of your investment.

In conclusion, identifying your target audience is a critical step in affiliate marketing. By understanding the needs, preferences, and behaviors of your audience, you can tailor your marketing strategies to effectively reach and engage them. Remember to continuously analyze and refine your approach based on data and feedback to maximize your chances of earning a six-figure income per month.

2.3 Evaluating Competition

When it comes to choosing profitable affiliate niches, one crucial aspect that you need to consider is evaluating the competition. Understanding the level of competition in your chosen niche is essential for your success as an affiliate marketer. By evaluating the competition, you can determine whether it is feasible to enter a particular niche and devise strategies to stand out from your competitors.

Understanding Competition Analysis

Competition analysis involves researching and analyzing the existing players in your chosen niche. It helps you gain insights into their strategies, strengths, weaknesses, and overall market dynamics. By evaluating the competition, you can identify opportunities and challenges that lie ahead, allowing you to make informed decisions about your affiliate marketing approach.

Steps to Evaluate Competition

To effectively evaluate the competition in your chosen niche, follow these steps:

1. Identify Competitors

Start by identifying your main competitors in the niche. Look for websites, blogs, and social media accounts that are already established and successful in promoting products or services related to your niche. Make a list of these competitors, as you will be analyzing their strategies and presence in the market.

2. Analyze Website Traffic

One of the key indicators of a competitor's success is their website traffic. Use tools like SimilarWeb or SEMrush to analyze the estimated traffic of your competitors' websites. This will give you an idea of how popular their sites are and the potential reach they have in the market.

3. Assess Social Media Presence

Social media platforms play a significant role in affiliate marketing. Evaluate your competitors' social media presence by examining the number of followers, engagement rates, and the quality of their content. This analysis will help you understand how well they are connecting with their target audience and the strategies they are using to drive traffic and engagement.

4. Study Content Strategy

Content is king in the world of affiliate marketing. Analyze the type of content your competitors are producing, such as blog posts, videos, or podcasts. Look for the topics they cover, the quality of their content, and how they engage with their audience. This analysis will help you identify gaps in their content strategy that you can fill with your unique approach.

5. Evaluate SEO Efforts

Search engine optimization (SEO) is crucial for driving organic traffic to your website. Assess your competitors' SEO efforts by analyzing their keyword rankings, backlink profiles, and on-page optimization. This analysis will give you insights into the keywords they are targeting and the strategies they are using to rank higher in search engine results.

6. Examine Affiliate Partnerships

Affiliate partnerships are an integral part of the affiliate marketing ecosystem. Research the affiliate programs your competitors are associated with and the products or services they promote. Look for opportunities to collaborate with similar affiliate programs or identify gaps where you can promote different products or services to diversify your income streams.

7. Consider Pricing and Offers

Evaluate the pricing and offers provided by your competitors. Analyze their pricing structure, discounts, and promotions. This analysis will help you understand the market dynamics and identify opportunities to offer competitive pricing or unique value propositions to attract customers.

8. Assess Customer Reviews and Feedback

Customer reviews and feedback provide valuable insights into the strengths and weaknesses of your competitors. Analyze the reviews and feedback left by customers on your competitors' websites, social media platforms, and review sites. This analysis will help you understand the pain points of customers and identify areas where you can provide better solutions or experiences.

Leveraging Competition Analysis

Once you have evaluated the competition, you can leverage the insights gained to develop a competitive advantage in your affiliate marketing efforts. Here are some strategies to consider:

Identify the unique selling points that set you apart from your competitors. Use this information to develop a strong brand identity and value proposition. Differentiate yourself by offering unique content, personalized recommendations, exceptional customer service, or exclusive deals.

If the competition in your chosen niche is intense, consider targeting specific subsegments within the niche. By focusing on a narrower audience, you can tailor your content and promotions to meet their specific needs and preferences. This approach allows you to establish yourself as an expert in a niche subsegment and attract a loyal following.

Collaborate with Complementary Affiliates

Instead of viewing other affiliates as competitors, consider collaborating with them. Look for affiliates who promote complementary products or services and explore opportunities for cross-promotion or joint ventures. By leveraging each other's audiences, you can expand your reach and increase your chances of success.

Offer Unique Value

Identify gaps in the market that your competitors have overlooked. Find ways to offer unique value to your audience, such as exclusive discounts, bonus content, or personalized recommendations. By providing something that others don't, you can attract and retain customers who are looking for a distinct experience.

Continuously Monitor and Adapt

Competition in the affiliate marketing industry is constantly evolving. Stay updated with industry trends, monitor your competitors' strategies, and adapt your approach accordingly. Continuously test and tweak your marketing strategies to stay ahead of the competition and maximize your affiliate marketing success.

Conclusion

Evaluating the competition is a crucial step in choosing profitable affiliate niches. By understanding your competitors' strategies, strengths, and weaknesses, you can develop a unique approach that sets you apart in the market. Use the insights gained from competition analysis to differentiate your brand, target niche subsegments, collaborate with complementary affiliates, offer unique value, and continuously adapt to stay ahead of the competition.

2.4 Selecting the Right Affiliate Programs

Choosing the right affiliate programs is crucial for your success in affiliate marketing. Not all programs are created equal, and selecting the right ones can make a significant difference in your ability to earn a six-figure income. In this section, we will discuss the key factors to consider when selecting affiliate programs and provide you with practical tips to help you make informed decisions.

Before we dive into the selection process, let's briefly recap what affiliate programs are. An affiliate program is a partnership between a merchant or product creator and an affiliate marketer. As an affiliate marketer, you promote the merchant's products or services and earn a commission for every sale or action generated through your referral.

Affiliate programs come in various forms, including individual affiliate programs run by product creators or merchants, as well as affiliate networks that act as intermediaries between affiliates and merchants. Affiliate networks, such as Amazon Associates, ClickBank, and Commission Junction, offer a wide range of products and services from different merchants, making it easier for affiliates to find suitable programs.

When selecting affiliate programs, your primary goal is to find programs that offer high earning potential. Here are some key factors to consider:

1. **Commission Structure:** Look for programs that offer generous commission rates. Higher commission rates mean you can earn more money per sale or action. Compare the commission rates of different programs within your niche and choose the ones that offer the best returns.

2. **Product Quality and Relevance:** It's essential to promote products or services that are of high quality and relevant to your target audience. If you promote low-quality or irrelevant products, your audience may lose trust in your recommendations, leading to lower conversions and earnings. Take the time to research and evaluate the products or services offered by the affiliate programs you are considering.

3. **Cookie Duration:** The cookie duration refers to the length of time a cookie (a small piece of data stored on the user's browser) remains active after a user clicks on your affiliate link. A longer cookie duration gives you a higher chance of earning a commission if the user makes a purchase within that timeframe. Look for programs with longer cookie durations to maximize your earning potential.

4. **Conversion Rate:** The conversion rate is the percentage of visitors who take the desired action, such as making a purchase or signing up for a service. Programs with higher conversion rates indicate that the product or service is appealing to customers and has a higher likelihood of generating sales.

Research the conversion rates of different affiliate programs to identify the ones with the best performance.

5. **Affiliate Support and Resources:** Consider the level of support and resources provided by the affiliate program. Some programs offer dedicated affiliate managers, marketing materials, and training resources to help you succeed. Having access to these resources can significantly impact your ability to generate sales and earn a six-figure income.

Now that you understand the key factors to consider, here are some practical tips to help you select the right affiliate programs:

1. **Research and Compare:** Take the time to research and compare different affiliate programs within your niche. Look for programs that align with your target audience's interests and needs. Compare commission rates, cookie durations, and conversion rates to identify the programs that offer the best earning potential.

2. **Read Reviews and Testimonials:** Look for reviews and testimonials from other affiliates who have experience with the programs you are considering. Their insights can provide valuable information about the program's performance, support, and overall satisfaction.

3. **Consider Your Audience's Needs:** Put yourself in your audience's shoes and consider what products or services would be most valuable to them. Choose affiliate programs that offer solutions to their problems or fulfill their desires. By promoting products that genuinely benefit your audience, you increase your chances of earning higher commissions.

4. **Evaluate the Merchant's Reputation:** Research the reputation of the merchant or product creator associated with the affiliate program. Look for signs of credibility, such as positive customer reviews, a strong brand presence, and a history of delivering quality products or services. Promoting products from reputable merchants enhances your own credibility as an affiliate marketer.

5. **Track and Analyze Performance:** Once you have selected affiliate programs and started promoting their products, track and analyze your performance. Monitor your sales, conversion rates, and earnings to identify which programs are delivering the best results. This data will help you optimize your efforts and focus on the most profitable programs.

Remember, selecting the right affiliate programs is an ongoing process. As your business grows and evolves, you may need to reassess and adjust your affiliate partnerships to maximize your earning potential. Stay informed about industry trends and new opportunities to ensure you are always promoting the most profitable programs.

By carefully selecting the right affiliate programs, you can increase your chances of earning a six-figure income per month. Combine this with effective marketing strategies, high-converting websites, and targeted traffic, and you'll be well on your way to affiliate marketing mastery.

Building a High-Converting Website

3.1 Choosing a Domain Name

Choosing a domain name is a crucial step in building a successful affiliate marketing website. Your domain name is essentially your online identity, and it plays a significant role in attracting visitors, establishing credibility, and improving search engine rankings. In this section, we will discuss the key factors to consider when choosing a domain name for your affiliate marketing business.

Importance of a Domain Name

A domain name is the web address that users will type into their browsers to access your website. It is essential to choose a domain name that is memorable, relevant to your niche, and easy to spell. A well-chosen domain name can help you stand out from the competition and make a lasting impression on your target audience.

Branding and Relevance

When selecting a domain name, it is crucial to consider your brand and the niche you are targeting. Your domain name should reflect the nature of your business and resonate with your target audience. It should be relevant, descriptive, and memorable. For example, if you are promoting fitness products, a domain name like "FitLifePro.com" would be more relevant and appealing than a generic name like "BestProductsOnline.com."

Keyword Research

Keyword research is an essential aspect of choosing a domain name. Conducting thorough keyword research will help you identify popular search terms related to your niche. By incorporating relevant keywords into your domain name, you can improve your website's visibility in search engine results. However, it is important to strike a balance between incorporating keywords and maintaining a brandable domain name. Avoid stuffing your domain name with too many keywords, as it can make it sound unnatural and spammy.

Domain Extensions

Domain extensions, also known as top-level domains (TLDs), are the suffixes that appear at the end of a domain name, such as .com, .net, or .org. The most common and widely recognized domain extension is .com. It is generally recommended to choose a .com domain if it is available, as it is more familiar to users and carries a sense of credibility. However, if a .com domain is not available for your desired name, you can consider other relevant extensions such as .net or .org.

Length and Simplicity

Short and simple domain names are generally easier to remember and type. Avoid using long and complex domain names that can confuse or frustrate users. Aim for a domain name that is concise, easy to spell, and pronounceable. This will make it easier for users to share your website with others and increase the chances of them returning to your site in the future.

Avoid Trademark Infringement

When choosing a domain name, it is crucial to ensure that you are not infringing on any trademarks. Conduct a thorough search to ensure that your chosen domain name does not violate any existing trademarks or copyrights. Using a trademarked name can lead to legal issues and damage your reputation. It is always better to be safe than sorry, so take the time to research and verify the availability of your chosen domain name.

Registering Your Domain Name

Once you have chosen the perfect domain name for your affiliate marketing website, it is time to register it. There are numerous domain registrars available where you can purchase and register your domain name. Some popular domain registrars include GoDaddy, Namecheap, and Bluehost. Compare prices and features offered by different registrars to find the best option for your needs.

Conclusion

Choosing a domain name is a critical step in building a successful affiliate marketing website. It is important to select a domain name that is relevant, memorable, and reflects your brand and niche. Conduct thorough keyword research, consider the length and simplicity of the domain name, and avoid trademark infringement. By following these guidelines, you can choose a domain name that will help you establish a strong online presence and attract your target audience.

3.2 Setting Up Web Hosting

Setting up web hosting is an essential step in building a high-converting website for your affiliate marketing business. Web hosting is the service that allows your website to be accessible on the internet. It provides the storage space and server resources needed to store your website files and make them available to visitors.

When it comes to setting up web hosting for your affiliate marketing website, there are a few key factors to consider. These factors include reliability, speed, security, customer support, and cost. In this section, we will explore the steps you need to take to set up web hosting for your affiliate marketing website and provide recommendations for affordable options.

The first step in setting up web hosting is to choose the right web hosting provider. There are numerous web hosting companies available, each offering different features and pricing plans. It's important to select a reliable and reputable provider that meets your specific needs.

When evaluating web hosting providers, consider the following factors:

1. **Reliability**: Look for a provider that offers a high uptime guarantee, ideally 99.9% or higher. This ensures that your website will be accessible to visitors at all times.

2. **Speed**: Website loading speed is crucial for user experience and search engine optimization. Choose a web hosting provider that offers fast server response times and utilizes caching technologies.

3. **Security**: Protecting your website and visitors' data is essential. Ensure that the web hosting provider offers robust security measures, such as SSL certificates, firewalls, and regular backups.

4. **Customer Support**: In case you encounter any technical issues or have questions, reliable customer support is crucial. Look for a web hosting provider that offers 24/7 support through various channels, such as live chat, phone, or email.

5. **Cost**: As a beginner affiliate marketer, it's important to find a web hosting provider that offers affordable pricing plans. Look for providers that offer competitive pricing without compromising on quality.

Here are a few web hosting providers that are known for their reliability, affordability, and excellent customer support:

1. **Bluehost**: Bluehost is a popular web hosting provider recommended by WordPress. They offer a range of hosting plans suitable for beginners, including shared hosting, which is a cost-effective option. Bluehost provides a free domain name for the first year and offers a user-friendly interface for easy website management.

2. **SiteGround**: SiteGround is another reputable web hosting provider known for its excellent performance and customer support. They offer various hosting options, including shared hosting, cloud hosting, and dedicated servers. SiteGround provides free SSL certificates, daily backups, and advanced security features.

3. **HostGator**: HostGator is a well-established web hosting provider that offers affordable hosting plans suitable for beginners. They provide a user-friendly control panel, 24/7 customer support, and a 45-day money-back guarantee. HostGator offers shared hosting, cloud hosting, and WordPress hosting options.

4. **DreamHost**: DreamHost is a reliable web hosting provider that offers a range of hosting plans, including shared hosting, VPS hosting, and dedicated servers. They provide a 97-day money-back guarantee, free SSL certificates, and unlimited bandwidth. DreamHost also offers a user-friendly website builder for beginners.

Setting Up Web Hosting

Once you have chosen a web hosting provider, follow these steps to set up your web hosting:

1. **Sign up for an account**: Visit the web hosting provider's website and sign up for an account. Choose the hosting plan that best suits your needs and budget.

2. **Register a domain name**: If you haven't already registered a domain name, most web hosting providers offer the option to register one during the sign-up process. Alternatively, you can register a domain name separately and connect it to your web hosting account.

3. **Configure your hosting account**: After signing up, you will receive login credentials to access your hosting account. Log in to your account and configure the necessary settings, such as setting up your domain, creating email accounts, and managing your website files.

4. **Install a content management system (CMS)**: Many web hosting providers offer one-click installation of popular CMS platforms like WordPress. Install your preferred CMS to easily manage and update your website content.

5. **Upload your website files**: If you have already designed your website, upload your website files to the server using an FTP client or the file manager provided by your web hosting provider.

6. **Set up email accounts**: If you want to have a professional email address associated with your domain, set up email accounts through your hosting provider's control panel.

7. **Test your website**: Once your website files are uploaded, test your website to ensure everything is functioning correctly. Check for any broken links, slow loading times, or other issues that may affect user experience.

Congratulations! You have successfully set up web hosting for your affiliate marketing website. Now you can move on to the next steps in building a high-converting website, such as designing an attractive website, creating engaging content, and optimizing for search engines.

Remember, choosing a reliable web hosting provider is crucial for the success of your affiliate marketing business. Take the time to research and compare different providers to find the one that best suits your needs and budget.

3.3 Designing an Attractive Website

Your website is the foundation of your affiliate marketing business. It is the platform where you will showcase your affiliate products, engage with your audience, and ultimately drive conversions. Designing an attractive website is crucial to capturing the attention of your visitors and keeping them engaged. In this section, we will explore the key elements of designing an attractive website that will help you maximize your affiliate marketing success.

1. Choose a Clean and Professional Design

When it comes to designing your website, simplicity is key. Choose a clean and professional design that is visually appealing and easy to navigate. Avoid cluttered layouts and excessive use of colors or graphics that can distract your visitors. Remember, the goal is to create a user-friendly experience that encourages visitors to stay on your site and explore further.

2. Use High-Quality Images and Graphics

Visual content plays a significant role in capturing the attention of your audience. Incorporate high-quality images and graphics that are relevant to your niche and products. Use visually appealing banners and product images to showcase your affiliate offerings. Ensure that the images are optimized for web use to maintain fast loading times and a seamless user experience.

3. Create a Clear and Compelling Call-to-Action

A call-to-action (CTA) is a crucial element of your website design. It is the prompt that encourages your visitors to take the desired action, such as making a purchase or signing up for a newsletter. Design a clear and compelling CTA that stands out on your website. Use contrasting colors and persuasive language to entice your visitors to click on the CTA button.

4. Implement Responsive Web Design

With the increasing use of mobile devices, it is essential to ensure that your website is responsive and mobile-friendly. Responsive web design allows your website to adapt to different screen sizes, providing a seamless browsing experience for your visitors across all devices. This is crucial as mobile traffic continues to grow, and search engines prioritize mobile-friendly websites in their rankings.

5. Optimize Website Speed

Website speed is a critical factor in user experience and search engine optimization. A slow-loading website can lead to high bounce rates and lower search engine rankings. Optimize your website speed by compressing images, minifying code, and leveraging caching techniques. Regularly monitor your website's speed using tools like Google PageSpeed Insights and make necessary optimizations to ensure a fast and smooth browsing experience.

6. Create Engaging and Relevant Content

Content is king in the world of affiliate marketing. Along with an attractive design, your website should offer valuable and engaging content that resonates with your target audience. Create informative blog posts, product reviews, and other types of content that provide value to your visitors. Incorporate relevant keywords to improve your search engine rankings and attract organic traffic.

7. Incorporate Social Proof

Social proof is a powerful tool in building trust and credibility with your audience. Incorporate testimonials, reviews, and success stories from satisfied customers on your website. Display social media follower counts and engagement metrics to showcase your popularity and influence. Social proof helps to establish your authority in your niche and encourages visitors to trust your recommendations.

8. Ensure Easy Navigation

A well-structured and intuitive navigation menu is essential for guiding your visitors through your website. Make sure your menu is easy to find and understand. Organize your content into logical categories and subcategories, allowing visitors to quickly find the information they are looking for. Implement a search bar to further enhance navigation and make it easier for visitors to find specific content.

9. Optimize for Search Engines

Search engine optimization (SEO) is crucial for driving organic traffic to your website. Optimize your website by incorporating relevant keywords in your content, meta tags, and URLs. Build high-quality backlinks from reputable websites to improve your search engine rankings. Regularly monitor your website's SEO performance and make necessary adjustments to stay ahead of the competition.

10. Test and Analyze

Designing an attractive website is an ongoing process. Continuously test different design elements, layouts, and content to optimize your website's performance. Use analytics tools like Google Analytics to track user behavior, conversion rates, and other key metrics. Analyze the data and make data-driven decisions to improve your website's effectiveness and maximize your affiliate marketing success.

Remember, an attractive website is just the beginning. It is essential to consistently update and improve your website to stay relevant and competitive in the ever-evolving world of affiliate marketing. By implementing the strategies outlined in this section, you will be well on your way to designing an attractive website that captivates your audience and drives conversions.

3.4 Creating Engaging Content

Creating engaging content is a crucial aspect of building a successful affiliate marketing website. Your content is what will attract and engage your audience, ultimately leading them to take action and make a purchase through your affiliate links. In this section, we will explore various strategies and techniques to help you create compelling and engaging content that drives conversions.

Understanding Your Target Audience

Before you start creating content, it's essential to have a deep understanding of your target audience. Who are they? What are their interests, needs, and pain points? By understanding your audience, you can tailor your content to resonate with them and provide value.

To gain insights into your target audience, conduct thorough research. Use tools like Google Analytics, social media analytics, and keyword research tools to gather data about your audience's demographics, interests, and online behavior. Additionally, engage with your audience through surveys, polls, and comments to gather direct feedback.

Choosing the Right Content Formats

Different people consume content in different ways. Some prefer reading blog posts, while others prefer watching videos or listening to podcasts. To cater to a broader audience, consider diversifying your content formats.

Blog posts are a popular and effective way to provide in-depth information and engage with your audience. Write informative and well-researched articles that address your audience's pain points and provide solutions. Use a conversational tone and include relevant visuals to make your content more engaging.

Videos are another powerful content format that can captivate your audience. Create video tutorials, product reviews, or interviews with industry experts. Videos allow you to showcase products and demonstrate their benefits effectively. Remember to optimize your videos for search engines by using relevant keywords in titles, descriptions, and tags.

Podcasts are gaining popularity as a convenient way for people to consume content while on the go. Consider starting a podcast where you discuss industry trends, interview experts, and provide valuable insights to your audience. Make sure to promote your affiliate products within the podcast episodes naturally.

Infographics are visually appealing and can convey complex information in a concise and engaging manner. Create infographics that highlight key points, statistics, or comparisons related to your niche. Share these infographics on your website and social media platforms to attract attention and drive traffic.

Crafting Compelling Headlines

Your headline is the first thing that grabs your audience's attention. It should be compelling, concise, and convey the value of your content. A well-crafted headline can significantly impact the click-through rate and engagement of your content.

Use power words and emotional triggers in your headlines to evoke curiosity and interest. Make it clear what your audience will gain by reading or watching your content. Experiment with different headline formulas and test their performance to find what works best for your audience.

Providing Valuable and Actionable Information

To engage your audience and build trust, your content should provide valuable and actionable information. Focus on solving your audience's problems and addressing their pain points. Offer practical tips, step-by-step guides, and actionable advice that they can implement immediately.

Back up your claims with evidence and include real-life examples to make your content more relatable. Use storytelling techniques to captivate your audience and make your content memorable. Incorporate relevant statistics, case studies, and expert opinions to add credibility to your content.

Incorporating Visuals and Multimedia

Visuals play a crucial role in engaging your audience and making your content more appealing. Use high-quality images, infographics, charts, and videos to break up text and make your content visually appealing. Visuals can help convey information more effectively and enhance the overall user experience.

Additionally, consider incorporating interactive elements into your content. Use quizzes, polls, and surveys to encourage audience participation and make your content more interactive. This not only increases engagement but also provides valuable insights into your audience's preferences and opinions.

Encouraging Audience Interaction

Engaging content should encourage audience interaction and foster a sense of community. Encourage your audience to leave comments, ask questions, and share their experiences. Respond to comments promptly and engage in conversations with your audience to build relationships and establish trust.

Consider creating a forum or community platform where your audience can connect with each other and share their thoughts and experiences. This not only increases engagement but also creates a sense of belonging and loyalty among your audience.

Optimizing for SEO

Creating engaging content is not enough; you also need to ensure that your content is discoverable by search engines. Implementing search engine optimization (SEO) techniques can help improve your content's visibility and drive organic traffic to your website.

Research and use relevant keywords in your content, including in titles, headings, and throughout the body. Optimize your meta tags, URLs, and image alt tags to make it easier for search engines to understand and index your content. Additionally, focus on creating high-quality backlinks from reputable websites to improve your website's authority and search engine rankings.

Conclusion

Creating engaging content is a fundamental aspect of successful affiliate marketing. By understanding your target audience, choosing the right content formats, crafting compelling headlines, providing valuable information, incorporating visuals, encouraging audience interaction, optimizing for SEO, and continuously testing and improving your content, you can create content that captivates your audience and drives conversions. Remember, engaging content is not a one-time effort but an ongoing process that requires constant refinement and adaptation to meet the changing needs and preferences of your audience.

3.5 Optimizing for Search Engines

Search engine optimization (SEO) is a crucial aspect of building a successful affiliate marketing business. By optimizing your website for search engines, you can increase your visibility in search results and attract organic traffic to your site. This section will guide you through the process of optimizing your website for search engines, helping you improve your rankings and drive more targeted traffic to your affiliate offers.

Understanding the Basics of SEO

Before diving into the strategies and techniques of SEO, it's important to understand the basics. Search engines like Google use complex algorithms to determine the relevance and quality of websites, and they rank them accordingly in search results. SEO involves optimizing your website to meet the criteria set by search engines, making it more likely to appear higher in search results.

The two main components of SEO are on-page optimization and off-page optimization. On-page optimization refers to optimizing the content and structure of your website, while off-page optimization involves building backlinks and establishing your website's authority in the online space.

Keyword research is the foundation of any successful SEO strategy. It involves identifying the keywords and phrases that your target audience is using to search for information related to your niche. By targeting these keywords in your content, you can increase your chances of ranking higher in search results.

Start by brainstorming a list of relevant keywords and phrases that are related to your niche. Use keyword research tools like Google Keyword Planner, SEMrush, or Ahrefs to expand your list and find additional keyword ideas. Look for keywords with a high search volume and low competition to maximize your chances of ranking well.

Once you have a list of keywords, strategically incorporate them into your website's content. Include them in your page titles, headings, meta descriptions, and throughout your website's copy. However, be careful not to overuse keywords, as this can be seen as spammy by search engines and negatively impact your rankings.

On-page optimization involves optimizing the content and structure of your website to make it more search engine-friendly. Here are some key on-page optimization techniques to implement:

1. **Optimize your website's structure**: Ensure that your website has a clear and logical structure, with easy navigation and user-friendly URLs. Use descriptive and keyword-rich URLs for your pages.

2. **Create high-quality content**: Develop informative and engaging content that provides value to your audience. Use your target keywords naturally throughout your content, but prioritize creating content that is helpful and relevant.

3. **Optimize your page titles and meta descriptions**: Craft compelling and keyword-rich page titles and meta descriptions for each page of your website. These elements appear in search results and can significantly impact click-through rates.

4. **Use header tags**: Utilize header tags (H1, H2, H3, etc.) to structure your content and make it easier for search engines to understand. Include your target keywords in your headers to signal the relevance of your content.

5. **Optimize your images**: Compress and resize your images to improve page load speed. Use descriptive file names and alt tags to help search engines understand the content of your images.

6. **Improve page load speed**: Optimize your website's performance by minimizing code, leveraging browser caching, and using a content delivery

network (CDN) if necessary. A fast-loading website improves user experience and can positively impact your search rankings.

Off-Page Optimization

Off-page optimization focuses on building your website's authority and credibility in the online space. The primary off-page optimization technique is building high-quality backlinks from reputable websites. Here are some strategies to consider:

1. **Guest blogging**: Write informative and valuable guest posts for other websites in your niche. Include a link back to your website in your author bio or within the content itself. Guest blogging not only helps you build backlinks but also exposes your brand to a wider audience.

2. **Social media promotion**: Share your content on social media platforms to increase its visibility and encourage others to link back to it. Engage with your audience and build relationships with influencers in your niche to expand your reach.

3. **Influencer outreach**: Reach out to influencers in your niche and offer to collaborate on content or promotions. When influencers mention or link to your website, it can significantly boost your credibility and authority.

4. **Directory submissions**: Submit your website to relevant directories and industry-specific listings. This can help improve your website's visibility and generate valuable backlinks.

5. **Monitor and manage your backlink profile**: Regularly monitor your backlinks to ensure they are from reputable sources. Disavow any low-quality or spammy backlinks that could harm your website's rankings.

Monitoring and Analytics

To track the effectiveness of your SEO efforts, it's essential to monitor your website's performance using analytics tools. Google Analytics is a popular choice and provides valuable insights into your website's traffic, user behavior, and conversion rates. Pay attention to key metrics such as organic traffic, bounce rate, average session duration, and conversion rates.

Regularly analyze your website's performance and make data-driven decisions to optimize your SEO strategy. Identify areas for improvement, experiment with different techniques, and continuously refine your approach to achieve better results.

By implementing effective SEO strategies, you can improve your website's visibility in search results and attract targeted organic traffic. Remember that SEO is an ongoing process, and it takes time to see significant results. Stay consistent, adapt to algorithm changes, and continuously optimize your website to maximize your chances of earning a six-figure income through affiliate marketing.

3.6 Implementing Conversion Optimization Strategies

In order to maximize your affiliate marketing income and achieve a six-figure income per month, it is crucial to implement effective conversion optimization strategies. Conversion optimization refers to the process of improving the percentage of website visitors who take a desired action, such as making a purchase or signing up for a newsletter. By optimizing your conversion rates, you can increase your affiliate sales and ultimately boost your income.

3.6.1 Conduct A/B Testing

One of the most effective ways to optimize your conversion rates is through A/B testing. A/B testing involves creating two versions of a webpage or a specific element on your website and testing them against each other to determine which version performs better. By testing different variations of your website, you can identify the elements that resonate most with your audience and lead to higher conversion rates.

When conducting A/B tests, it is important to focus on one element at a time. For example, you can test different headlines, call-to-action buttons, or color schemes. By isolating specific elements, you can accurately measure the impact of each variation on your conversion rates. It is also important to track and analyze the results of your tests to make data-driven decisions and continuously improve your website's performance.

3.6.2 Optimize Website Speed

Website speed plays a crucial role in conversion optimization. Research has shown that even a one-second delay in page load time can significantly impact conversion rates. Slow-loading websites can lead to higher bounce rates, lower engagement, and ultimately, fewer sales. Therefore, it is essential to optimize your website's speed to provide a seamless user experience and increase the likelihood of conversions.

To optimize your website's speed, you can start by minimizing the size of your images and optimizing their format. Compressing images and using the appropriate file format can significantly reduce loading times. Additionally, you can leverage browser caching, enable file compression, and minimize the use of external scripts and plugins. Regularly monitoring your website's speed using tools like Google PageSpeed Insights can help you identify areas for improvement and ensure optimal performance.

3.6.3 Improve Website Design and User Experience

The design and user experience of your website play a crucial role in conversion optimization. A visually appealing and user-friendly website can significantly impact your conversion rates. When visitors land on your website, they should be able to navigate easily, find the information they need, and have a seamless browsing experience.

To improve your website's design and user experience, consider the following strategies:

- Simplify navigation: Ensure that your website's navigation is intuitive and easy to understand. Use clear and concise menu labels and organize your content in a logical manner.
- Use compelling visuals: Incorporate high-quality images and videos that are relevant to your affiliate products or services. Visuals can capture visitors' attention and increase engagement.
- Optimize for mobile devices: With the increasing use of mobile devices, it is crucial to have a responsive website design that adapts to different screen sizes. Mobile optimization can improve user experience and increase conversions.
- Streamline the checkout process: If you are promoting products that require a purchase, make sure the checkout process is simple and streamlined. Minimize the number of steps and eliminate any unnecessary fields or distractions.

By continuously improving your website's design and user experience, you can create a positive impression on visitors and increase the likelihood of conversions.

3.6.4 Use Persuasive Call-to-Actions

A persuasive call-to-action (CTA) is a crucial element in conversion optimization. A well-crafted CTA can encourage visitors to take the desired action, whether it's making a purchase, signing up for a newsletter, or downloading a resource. To optimize your CTAs, consider the following tips:

- Use action-oriented language: Use verbs that prompt action, such as "Buy Now," "Sign Up," or "Download."
- Create a sense of urgency: Incorporate words or phrases that create a sense of urgency, such as "Limited Time Offer" or "Only X Spots Left."
- Make CTAs visually prominent: Use contrasting colors, larger font sizes, or buttons to make your CTAs stand out on the page.
- Test different variations: A/B test different versions of your CTAs to determine which ones generate the highest conversion rates.

By optimizing your CTAs, you can effectively guide visitors towards the desired action and increase your affiliate sales.

3.6.5 Leverage Social Proof

Social proof is a powerful conversion optimization strategy that involves showcasing positive feedback, testimonials, or reviews from satisfied customers. When visitors see that others have had a positive experience with your affiliate products or services, they are more likely to trust your recommendations and make a purchase.

To leverage social proof, consider the following tactics:

- Display customer testimonials: Incorporate testimonials from satisfied customers on your website. Include their name, photo, and any relevant details that add credibility.
- Showcase user-generated content: Encourage customers to share their experiences with your products or services on social media. You can then feature this content on your website to build trust and credibility.
- Highlight positive reviews: If your affiliate products or services have received positive reviews on external platforms, showcase them on your website. This can help build trust and influence purchasing decisions.

By leveraging social proof, you can build credibility and trust with your audience, ultimately leading to higher conversion rates.

Implementing these conversion optimization strategies can significantly improve your affiliate marketing performance and increase your chances of earning a six-figure income per month. Continuously testing, analyzing, and optimizing your website and marketing efforts will help you stay ahead of the competition and maximize your affiliate sales.

Driving Targeted Traffic to Your Website

4.1 Understanding Different Traffic Sources

In order to succeed in affiliate marketing and earn a six-figure income per month, it is crucial to understand the different sources of traffic that can drive visitors to your website. Traffic is the lifeblood of any online business, and without it, your affiliate marketing efforts will go unnoticed. By diversifying your traffic sources and implementing effective strategies, you can increase your chances of success and maximize your earning potential.

Organic Traffic

Organic traffic refers to the visitors who find your website through search engines like Google, Bing, or Yahoo. This type of traffic is highly valuable because it is free and targeted. When someone searches for a specific keyword or phrase related to your niche, and your website appears in the search results, there is a higher likelihood that they will be interested in the products or services you are promoting.

To generate organic traffic, you need to focus on search engine optimization (SEO). This involves optimizing your website's content, structure, and keywords to rank higher in search engine results pages (SERPs). By conducting keyword research and incorporating relevant keywords into your website's content, meta tags, and headings, you can increase your chances of appearing in search results and attracting organic traffic.

Pay-Per-Click (PPC) Advertising

PPC advertising is a paid traffic source where you pay for each click on your ads. This type of advertising allows you to display your ads on search engine results pages or other websites related to your niche. The most popular PPC advertising platform is Google Ads, which allows you to create ads and bid on keywords relevant to your affiliate products.

To effectively use PPC advertising, it is important to conduct thorough keyword research and create compelling ad copy that entices users to click on your ads. You should also optimize your landing pages to ensure a seamless user experience and increase the chances of conversion. It is crucial to monitor and analyze your PPC campaigns regularly to optimize your ad spend and maximize your return on investment (ROI).

Social Media Marketing

Social media platforms like Facebook, Instagram, Twitter, and LinkedIn offer immense opportunities for driving targeted traffic to your website. With billions of active users, social media platforms provide a vast audience to promote your affiliate products and engage with potential customers.

To leverage social media marketing effectively, you need to identify the platforms that are most relevant to your target audience. Each platform has its own unique features and user demographics, so it is important to tailor your content and marketing strategies accordingly. By creating engaging and shareable content, running targeted ad campaigns, and actively engaging with your audience, you can drive traffic to your website and increase your affiliate sales.

Email Marketing

Email marketing is a powerful tool for driving traffic and generating affiliate sales. By building an email list of subscribers who are interested in your niche, you can regularly communicate with them and promote your affiliate products. Email marketing allows you to establish a direct and personal connection with your audience, increasing the chances of conversion.

To build an email list, you need to offer valuable incentives, such as free e-books, exclusive content, or discounts, in exchange for visitors' email addresses. Once you have a list of subscribers, you can send them regular newsletters, product recommendations, and promotional offers. It is important to provide valuable content and avoid spamming your subscribers with excessive promotional emails. By nurturing and engaging your email list, you can drive targeted traffic to your website and increase your affiliate sales.

Content marketing involves creating and distributing valuable and relevant content to attract and engage your target audience. By providing informative and helpful content, you can establish yourself as an authority in your niche and build trust with your audience. Content marketing can take various forms, including blog posts, articles, videos, podcasts, infographics, and more.

To drive traffic through content marketing, you need to create high-quality and SEO-optimized content that addresses the needs and interests of your target audience. By conducting keyword research and incorporating relevant keywords into your content, you can increase your chances of ranking higher in search engine results and attracting organic traffic. It is also important to promote your content through social media, email marketing, and other channels to reach a wider audience and drive traffic to your website.

In conclusion, understanding the different sources of traffic is essential for achieving success in affiliate marketing and earning a six-figure income per month. By diversifying your traffic sources and implementing effective strategies, such as SEO, PPC advertising, social media marketing, email marketing, and content marketing, you can drive targeted traffic to your website and increase your affiliate sales. Remember to continuously monitor and analyze your traffic sources to optimize your strategies and maximize your earning potential.

4.2 Search Engine Optimization (SEO)

Search Engine Optimization (SEO) is a crucial aspect of driving targeted traffic to your affiliate website. By optimizing your website for search engines, you can increase your visibility in search engine results pages (SERPs) and attract organic traffic from people actively searching for the products or services you promote. In this section, we will explore the key strategies and techniques you can implement to improve your website's SEO and boost your affiliate marketing success.

Understanding the Basics of SEO

Before diving into the specific SEO strategies, it's essential to understand the basic principles behind search engine optimization. Search engines like Google use complex algorithms to determine the relevance and quality of websites, which ultimately affects their ranking in search results. By aligning your website with these algorithms, you can improve your chances of ranking higher and attracting more organic traffic.

The key elements of SEO include:

1. **Keyword Research**: Identifying the keywords and phrases that your target audience is using to search for products or services in your niche. This research helps you optimize your website's content to match these keywords and increase your visibility in search results.

2. **On-Page Optimization**: Optimizing various on-page elements of your website, such as meta tags, headings, URLs, and content, to make them more search engine-friendly. This includes incorporating relevant keywords naturally into your content and ensuring your website is well-structured and easy to navigate.

3. **Off-Page Optimization**: Building high-quality backlinks from reputable websites to improve your website's authority and credibility in the eyes of search engines. Off-page optimization also involves social media signals, brand mentions, and other factors that contribute to your website's overall reputation.

4. **Technical SEO**: Ensuring that your website is technically sound and optimized for search engines. This includes factors such as website speed, mobile-friendliness, site architecture, and proper indexing of your web pages.

Conducting Keyword Research

Keyword research is the foundation of any successful SEO strategy. By identifying the right keywords, you can optimize your website's content to match the search intent of your target audience. Here's how you can conduct effective keyword research:

1. **Brainstorm Relevant Topics**: Start by brainstorming a list of topics related to your niche. Think about the products or services you promote and the problems they solve. These topics will form the basis for your keyword research.

2. **Use Keyword Research Tools**: Utilize keyword research tools like Google Keyword Planner, SEMrush, or Ahrefs to discover relevant keywords and their search volumes. These tools provide insights into the popularity and competitiveness of keywords, helping you choose the most effective ones for your website.

3. **Analyze Competitor Keywords**: Study your competitors' websites and identify the keywords they are targeting. This can give you valuable insights into the keywords that are driving traffic to their websites and help you discover new keyword opportunities.

4. **Long-Tail Keywords**: Consider targeting long-tail keywords, which are longer and more specific phrases that have lower search volumes but higher conversion rates. Long-tail keywords often indicate a higher level of purchase intent and can help you attract more qualified traffic.

On-Page Optimization Techniques

Once you have identified your target keywords, it's time to optimize your website's on-page elements. Here are some key on-page optimization techniques to implement:

1. **Optimize Page Titles and Meta Descriptions**: Craft compelling and keyword-rich page titles and meta descriptions that accurately describe the content of each page. These elements appear in search results and can significantly impact click-through rates.

2. **Create High-Quality and Relevant Content**: Develop informative, engaging, and well-structured content that incorporates your target keywords naturally. Aim to provide value to your audience and answer their questions or solve their problems.

3. **Use Heading Tags**: Utilize heading tags (H1, H2, H3, etc.) to structure your content and make it easier for search engines to understand the hierarchy and relevance of different sections.

4. **Optimize Images**: Compress and optimize images to reduce their file size and improve page loading speed. Use descriptive alt tags to provide context to search engines and visually impaired users.

5. **Improve Website Speed**: Optimize your website's loading speed by minimizing code, leveraging browser caching, and using a content delivery network (CDN). A faster website not only improves user experience but also positively impacts search engine rankings.

Building High-Quality Backlinks

Off-page optimization plays a crucial role in SEO, and building high-quality backlinks is a key component of it. Backlinks are links from other websites that point to your website, indicating its authority and relevance. Here's how you can build high-quality backlinks:

1. **Guest Blogging**: Contribute guest posts to reputable websites in your niche. Include a link back to your website within the content or author bio. Guest blogging not only helps you build backlinks but also establishes you as an authority in your industry.

2. **Broken Link Building**: Identify broken links on other websites and reach out to the website owners, offering them a replacement link to your relevant and high-quality content.

3. **Social Media Promotion**: Share your content on social media platforms and engage with your audience. When your content gets shared and linked to from social media, it can improve your website's visibility and attract more backlinks.

4. **Influencer Outreach**: Collaborate with influencers in your niche and ask them to share your content or provide a backlink to your website. Influencers' endorsements can significantly boost your website's credibility and attract more organic traffic.

To ensure the effectiveness of your SEO efforts, it's crucial to monitor and analyze your website's performance regularly. Here are some key metrics to track:

1. **Organic Traffic**: Monitor the amount of organic traffic your website receives over time. Analyze the sources of traffic and identify the keywords that are driving the most traffic to your website.

2. **Keyword Rankings**: Keep track of your website's rankings for target keywords in search engine results. Identify any fluctuations and make necessary adjustments to your SEO strategy.

3. **Backlink Profile**: Monitor the number and quality of backlinks pointing to your website. Regularly check for any toxic or spammy backlinks and disavow them if necessary.

4. **Bounce Rate and Time on Page**: Analyze user behavior metrics like bounce rate and time on page to understand how engaged your visitors are with your content. Optimize your website's design and content to improve these metrics.

By implementing effective SEO strategies, you can improve your website's visibility, attract targeted organic traffic, and increase your chances of earning a six-figure income per month through affiliate marketing. Remember that SEO is an ongoing process, and it requires continuous monitoring, analysis, and adaptation to stay ahead of the competition and maintain long-term success.

4.3 Pay-Per-Click (PPC) Advertising

Pay-Per-Click (PPC) advertising is a powerful strategy that can help you drive targeted traffic to your affiliate website and increase your chances of earning a six-figure income per month. Unlike other forms of advertising, PPC allows you to only pay when someone clicks on your ad, making it a cost-effective method for generating leads and sales.

Understanding Pay-Per-Click (PPC) Advertising

PPC advertising is a model where advertisers pay a fee each time their ad is clicked. It is an auction-based system where advertisers bid on specific keywords relevant to their target audience. When a user searches for a keyword, the search engine displays relevant ads based on the bidding and quality score of the advertisers.

The two most popular PPC advertising platforms are Google Ads (formerly known as Google AdWords) and Bing Ads. These platforms allow you to create text-based ads that appear on search engine results pages when users search for specific keywords. Additionally, there are also display advertising networks like Google Display Network and social media platforms like Facebook Ads that offer PPC advertising options.

PPC advertising offers several benefits that make it an attractive option for affiliate marketers looking to earn a six-figure income per month:

1. **Immediate Results**: Unlike other marketing strategies that take time to generate results, PPC advertising can drive targeted traffic to your website almost instantly. As soon as your ads are approved, they can start appearing on search engine results pages, increasing your chances of making sales.

2. **Targeted Audience**: PPC advertising allows you to target specific keywords and demographics, ensuring that your ads are shown to the right audience. This targeting capability helps you reach potential customers who are actively searching for products or services related to your affiliate niche.

3. **Cost Control**: With PPC advertising, you have full control over your budget. You can set a daily or monthly budget and adjust it based on your needs. This flexibility allows you to optimize your spending and maximize your return on investment (ROI).

4. **Measurable Results**: PPC advertising provides detailed analytics and reporting, allowing you to track the performance of your ads. You can monitor metrics such as click-through rates (CTR), conversion rates, and cost per acquisition (CPA). This data helps you make informed decisions and optimize your campaigns for better results.

Getting Started with PPC Advertising

To start earning a six-figure income per month through PPC advertising, follow these steps:

1. **Keyword Research**: Begin by conducting thorough keyword research to identify the most relevant and high-converting keywords for your affiliate niche. Use keyword research tools like Google Keyword Planner, SEMrush, or Ahrefs to find keywords with high search volume and low competition.

2. **Create Compelling Ads**: Write compelling ad copy that grabs the attention of your target audience and entices them to click on your ads. Highlight the unique selling points of the products or services you are promoting and include a strong call-to-action (CTA) to encourage clicks.

3. **Set Up Landing Pages**: Create dedicated landing pages on your website that are optimized for the keywords you are targeting. These landing pages should provide valuable information and a clear path to conversion. Make sure your landing pages are mobile-friendly and have fast loading times to improve user experience.

4. **Bid Management**: Set your maximum bid for each keyword based on your budget and the estimated value of each click. Monitor your bids regularly and

adjust them based on the performance of your ads. Higher bids can help you secure top ad positions, but they may also increase your cost per click (CPC).

5. **Ad Testing and Optimization**: Continuously test different ad variations to identify the ones that perform best. Experiment with different headlines, ad copy, and CTAs to improve your click-through rates and conversion rates. Regularly review your campaign performance and make data-driven optimizations to maximize your ROI.

6. **Conversion Tracking**: Implement conversion tracking on your website to measure the effectiveness of your PPC campaigns. Set up conversion goals in your PPC advertising platform and track the number of conversions generated from your ads. This data will help you identify which keywords and ads are driving the most sales.

7. **Monitor and Refine**: Regularly monitor the performance of your PPC campaigns and make necessary adjustments. Analyze the data provided by your PPC platform and identify areas for improvement. Refine your keyword targeting, ad copy, and landing pages to optimize your campaigns for better results.

Remember, while PPC advertising can be highly effective, it requires careful planning, monitoring, and optimization to achieve a six-figure income per month. It is essential to continuously refine your strategies and adapt to changes in the market to stay ahead of the competition.

By leveraging the power of PPC advertising, you can drive targeted traffic to your affiliate website, increase your conversions, and ultimately achieve your income goals in affiliate marketing.

4.4 Social Media Marketing

Social media has become an integral part of our daily lives, and it presents a massive opportunity for affiliate marketers to reach a wider audience and drive targeted traffic to their websites. With billions of active users on platforms like Facebook, Instagram, Twitter, and LinkedIn, social media marketing has the potential to generate significant income for affiliate marketers. In this section, we will explore how you can leverage social media to maximize your affiliate marketing efforts and earn a six-figure income per month.

Understanding the Power of Social Media Marketing

Social media platforms offer a unique opportunity to connect with your target audience on a personal level. By creating engaging and valuable content, you can build a loyal following and establish yourself as an authority in your niche. Social media marketing allows you to leverage the power of word-of-mouth marketing, as users can easily share your content with their friends and followers, expanding your reach exponentially.

To effectively utilize social media for affiliate marketing, it's essential to choose the right platforms that align with your target audience. Conduct thorough research to identify which platforms your target audience is most active on. For example, if you're targeting a younger demographic, platforms like Instagram and TikTok may be more suitable, while LinkedIn might be better for a professional audience.

To succeed in social media marketing, you need to build a strong presence on the platforms you choose. Here are some key steps to follow:

1. **Optimize Your Profiles**: Ensure that your social media profiles are complete, professional, and aligned with your brand. Use high-quality images, write compelling bios, and include relevant links to your website or landing pages.

2. **Consistent Branding**: Maintain consistent branding across all your social media profiles. Use the same logo, color scheme, and tone of voice to create a cohesive brand image.

3. **Content Strategy**: Develop a content strategy that resonates with your target audience. Create a mix of informative, entertaining, and promotional content to keep your followers engaged. Use a variety of formats such as images, videos, and infographics to diversify your content.

4. **Engagement and Interaction**: Social media is all about building relationships. Engage with your followers by responding to comments, messages, and mentions. Encourage discussions, ask questions, and show genuine interest in your audience.

5. **Hashtags and Keywords**: Utilize relevant hashtags and keywords in your social media posts to increase visibility and reach. Research popular hashtags in your niche and incorporate them strategically into your content.

Once you have built a strong social media presence, it's time to start promoting your affiliate products. Here are some effective strategies to consider:

1. **Product Reviews**: Create detailed and honest product reviews that highlight the benefits and features of the affiliate products you are promoting. Use a mix of text, images, and videos to make your reviews engaging and informative.

2. **Giveaways and Contests**: Organize giveaways and contests on your social media platforms to generate excitement and engagement. Encourage participants to share your content and follow your page for a chance to win the prize. This can help increase your reach and attract new followers.

3. **Influencer Collaborations**: Collaborate with influencers in your niche to promote your affiliate products. Influencers have a loyal following and can help you reach a wider audience. Negotiate partnerships where they create content featuring your products and provide unique discount codes or affiliate links.

4. **Social Media Ads**: Consider running paid social media ads to target specific demographics and increase visibility for your affiliate products. Platforms like Facebook and Instagram offer robust advertising tools that allow you to target users based on their interests, demographics, and behaviors.

5. **Affiliate Links in Bio**: Many social media platforms allow you to include a link in your bio or profile description. Use this space to promote your affiliate products by including a compelling call-to-action and a trackable affiliate link.

Tracking and Analyzing Social Media Performance

To measure the effectiveness of your social media marketing efforts, it's crucial to track and analyze your performance. Here are some key metrics to monitor:

1. **Engagement**: Track the number of likes, comments, shares, and clicks your social media posts receive. This will help you understand which types of content resonate best with your audience.

2. **Conversion Rate**: Measure the number of clicks on your affiliate links and the subsequent conversions. This will give you insights into the effectiveness of your promotional efforts.

3. **Follower Growth**: Monitor the growth of your social media following over time. This metric indicates the success of your content strategy and the overall appeal of your brand.

4. **Referral Traffic**: Use analytics tools like Google Analytics to track the amount of traffic your social media platforms are driving to your website. This will help you understand the impact of your social media marketing on your overall website traffic.

By consistently monitoring and analyzing these metrics, you can identify areas for improvement and optimize your social media marketing strategy for maximum results.

Conclusion

Social media marketing is a powerful tool for affiliate marketers to drive targeted traffic, build brand awareness, and generate a six-figure income per month. By understanding the power of social media, choosing the right platforms, building a strong presence, and implementing effective promotional strategies, you can leverage social media to maximize your affiliate marketing efforts. Remember to track and analyze your performance to continuously improve and adapt your social media marketing strategy.

4.5 Email Marketing

Email marketing is a powerful tool that can significantly contribute to your success in affiliate marketing. It allows you to build a loyal audience, nurture relationships with potential customers, and drive targeted traffic to your affiliate offers. In this section, we will explore the strategies and techniques you can use to leverage email marketing and maximize your affiliate sales.

4.5.1 The Importance of Email Marketing

Email marketing is a highly effective way to communicate with your audience and build a long-term relationship with them. It allows you to directly reach out to your subscribers, deliver valuable content, and promote your affiliate products or services. Here are some key reasons why email marketing is crucial for your affiliate marketing success:

1. **Direct communication**: Unlike other marketing channels, email marketing allows you to have direct and personalized communication with your audience. You can tailor your messages to their specific needs and interests, increasing the chances of conversion.

2. **Building trust and credibility**: By consistently delivering valuable content and recommendations, you can establish yourself as an authority in your niche. This helps build trust and credibility with your subscribers, making them more likely to purchase products or services you recommend.

3. **Targeted audience**: With email marketing, you have the ability to segment your audience based on their interests, preferences, and behavior. This allows you to send targeted and relevant messages to specific groups, increasing the effectiveness of your campaigns.

4. **Cost-effective**: Email marketing is a cost-effective strategy compared to other marketing channels. With a small investment in an email marketing platform, you can reach a large number of subscribers and generate significant revenue.

4.5.2 Creating Lead Magnets

To build an email list, you need to offer something valuable in exchange for your visitors' email addresses. This is where lead magnets come into play. Lead magnets are free resources or incentives that you offer to your audience in exchange for their contact information. Here are some popular types of lead magnets you can create:

1. **Ebooks or guides**: Create a comprehensive ebook or guide that provides valuable information related to your niche. Make sure it addresses a specific problem or pain point your audience is facing.

2. **Checklists or cheat sheets**: Offer a checklist or cheat sheet that simplifies a complex process or provides a quick reference guide. This type of lead magnet is easy to consume and provides immediate value.

3. **Video tutorials or webinars**: Create video tutorials or host webinars where you share your expertise and provide actionable tips and strategies. This type of lead magnet allows you to showcase your knowledge and build trust with your audience.

4. **Templates or swipe files**: Provide ready-to-use templates or swipe files that your audience can use to save time and effort. This could include email templates, social media post templates, or design templates.

When creating lead magnets, it's important to ensure that they are highly relevant to your target audience and provide genuine value. This will increase the likelihood of visitors opting in to your email list.

4.5.3 Setting Up Email Marketing Campaigns

Once you have built your email list, it's time to set up email marketing campaigns to engage and nurture your subscribers. Here are the key steps to follow:

1. **Choose an email marketing platform**: There are several email marketing platforms available, such as Mailchimp, AWeber, and ConvertKit. Choose a platform that suits your needs and budget.

2. **Create an opt-in form**: Place opt-in forms on your website or landing pages to capture email addresses. Keep the form simple and ask for minimal information to increase conversion rates.

3. **Segment your audience**: Segment your email list based on factors such as interests, demographics, or purchase history. This allows you to send targeted emails that resonate with specific segments of your audience.

4. **Craft compelling email content**: Write engaging and valuable content for your emails. Provide useful information, share tips and strategies, and include relevant affiliate product recommendations.

5. **Automate your email sequences**: Set up automated email sequences or drip campaigns to deliver a series of emails to your subscribers over a specific period. This helps nurture relationships and guide subscribers through the buyer's journey.

6. **Monitor and analyze performance**: Track the performance of your email campaigns using analytics provided by your email marketing platform. Monitor open rates, click-through rates, and conversion rates to optimize your campaigns.

4.5.4 Nurturing and Engaging Subscribers

To maximize the effectiveness of your email marketing campaigns, it's important to nurture and engage your subscribers. Here are some strategies to consider:

1. **Provide valuable content**: Focus on delivering valuable content that educates, entertains, or solves a problem for your subscribers. This helps build trust and keeps your audience engaged.

2. **Personalize your emails**: Use personalization techniques to make your emails feel more personalized and relevant to each subscriber. Address them by their name and segment your emails based on their interests or preferences.

3. **Use storytelling**: Incorporate storytelling into your emails to create a connection with your subscribers. Share personal experiences, case studies, or success stories to make your emails more relatable and engaging.

4. **Include call-to-actions (CTAs)**: Encourage your subscribers to take action by including clear and compelling CTAs in your emails. Whether it's to click on a link, make a purchase, or share your content, make sure your CTAs are persuasive and easy to follow.

5. **Engage with your subscribers**: Encourage your subscribers to reply to your emails and engage in a conversation. Respond to their questions or comments promptly to show that you value their input.

By nurturing and engaging your subscribers, you can build a loyal audience that is more likely to convert into paying customers. Remember to always provide value and maintain a consistent email schedule to keep your audience engaged.

In conclusion, email marketing is a powerful tool that can significantly contribute to your success in affiliate marketing. By creating lead magnets, setting up email marketing campaigns, and nurturing your subscribers, you can build a loyal audience and drive targeted traffic to your affiliate offers. Remember to always provide valuable content, personalize your emails, and engage with your subscribers to maximize the effectiveness of your email marketing efforts.

4.6 Content Marketing

Content marketing is a powerful strategy that can help you drive targeted traffic to your website and increase your affiliate sales. By creating valuable and engaging content, you can attract and retain your target audience, establish yourself as an authority in your niche, and ultimately generate a six-figure income per month. In this section, we will explore the key principles and strategies of content marketing for affiliate marketers.

4.6.1 Understanding the Importance of Content Marketing

Content marketing is the process of creating and distributing valuable, relevant, and consistent content to attract and retain a clearly defined audience. It involves creating various types of content, such as blog posts, articles, videos, podcasts, infographics, and social media posts, that provide value to your target audience. By consistently delivering high-quality content, you can build trust, establish credibility, and develop a loyal following.

In the context of affiliate marketing, content marketing plays a crucial role in driving targeted traffic to your website. When you create valuable content that addresses the needs and interests of your target audience, you can attract organic traffic from search engines, social media platforms, and other online channels. This targeted traffic is more likely to convert into affiliate sales, resulting in a higher income potential.

4.6.2 Creating Valuable and Engaging Content

To succeed in content marketing, it is essential to create content that provides value to your audience and engages them. Here are some key strategies to create valuable and engaging content:

1. Understand Your Target Audience

Before creating content, it is crucial to understand your target audience. Research their needs, interests, pain points, and preferences. This will help you create content that resonates with them and provides solutions to their problems.

2. Provide Educational and Informative Content

Create content that educates and informs your audience. Share your knowledge, expertise, and insights to help them solve their problems or achieve their goals. This could include tutorials, guides, case studies, industry news, and expert interviews.

3. Use Storytelling Techniques

Storytelling is a powerful tool to engage your audience and make your content more memorable. Incorporate storytelling techniques into your content to captivate your audience's attention and create an emotional connection with them.

4. Use Visuals and Multimedia

Visuals and multimedia elements, such as images, videos, infographics, and podcasts, can enhance the appeal and effectiveness of your content. Use these elements strategically to convey your message and make your content more engaging.

5. Optimize Your Content for Search Engines

To attract organic traffic, optimize your content for search engines. Conduct keyword research to identify relevant keywords and incorporate them naturally into your content. Optimize your titles, headings, meta descriptions, and URLs to improve your search engine rankings.

6. Encourage User Interaction and Engagement

Encourage user interaction and engagement with your content. Include calls-to-action, such as asking for comments, feedback, or social media shares. Respond to comments and engage with your audience to build a sense of community and foster loyalty.

4.6.3 Content Distribution and Promotion

Creating valuable content is only half the battle. To maximize its impact, you need to distribute and promote your content effectively. Here are some strategies to distribute and promote your content:

1. Share on Social Media Platforms

Leverage social media platforms to distribute and promote your content. Share your content on platforms where your target audience is active, such as Facebook, Twitter, Instagram, LinkedIn, and Pinterest. Use relevant hashtags, engage with your audience, and encourage social sharing.

2. Guest Blogging

Guest blogging involves writing and publishing articles on other websites in your niche. This allows you to tap into the existing audience of those websites and drive traffic back to your own website. Look for reputable websites that accept guest posts and contribute high-quality content.

3. Email Marketing

Utilize your email list to distribute and promote your content. Send regular newsletters or updates to your subscribers, featuring your latest content. Include compelling headlines, snippets, and links to encourage click-throughs and engagement.

4. Influencer Outreach

Reach out to influencers in your niche and collaborate with them to promote your content. This could involve guest appearances on their podcasts, interviews, or joint content creation. Leveraging the reach and influence of established influencers can significantly boost the visibility and reach of your content.

5. Repurpose Your Content

Repurpose your content into different formats to reach a wider audience. For example, you can turn a blog post into a video, an infographic, or a podcast episode. This allows you to cater to different preferences and consumption habits of your audience.

4.6.4 Analyzing and Optimizing Your Content

To maximize the effectiveness of your content marketing efforts, it is crucial to analyze and optimize your content. Here are some key strategies to analyze and optimize your content:

1. Track Key Metrics

Use analytics tools to track key metrics, such as website traffic, engagement, conversion rates, and affiliate sales. This will help you identify the most successful content and understand what resonates with your audience.

2. A/B Testing

Conduct A/B testing to compare different versions of your content and determine which performs better. Test different headlines, formats, visuals, and calls-to-action to optimize your content for maximum impact.

3. Monitor Feedback and Comments

Pay attention to feedback and comments from your audience. Monitor social media conversations, comments on your blog posts, and emails from your subscribers. This feedback can provide valuable insights into what your audience likes and dislikes, helping you refine your content strategy.

4. Continuously Improve and Evolve

Content marketing is an ongoing process of continuous improvement. Stay up-to-date with industry trends, experiment with new formats and strategies, and continuously refine your content to meet the evolving needs and preferences of your audience.

By implementing these content marketing strategies, you can drive targeted traffic to your website, increase your affiliate sales, and ultimately achieve a six-figure income per month. Remember, consistency, quality, and value are the keys to success in content marketing.

Creating Compelling Affiliate Content

5.1 Writing Persuasive Product Reviews

One of the most effective ways to promote affiliate products and generate sales is through writing persuasive product reviews. Product reviews provide valuable information to potential buyers, helping them make informed decisions about whether or not to purchase a particular product. When done correctly, product reviews can be highly persuasive and drive significant affiliate sales. In this section, we will discuss the key elements of writing persuasive product reviews that can help you maximize your affiliate marketing income.

Understanding the Product

Before you can write a persuasive product review, it is crucial to have a deep understanding of the product you are promoting. Take the time to thoroughly research and familiarize yourself with the features, benefits, and drawbacks of the product. This will allow you to provide accurate and detailed information to your audience, building trust and credibility.

Highlighting the Benefits

When writing a product review, it is essential to focus on the benefits of the product. Highlight how the product can solve a problem or fulfill a need for your audience. Discuss the specific features that make the product unique and valuable. By emphasizing the benefits, you can create a sense of desire and urgency in your readers, increasing the likelihood of them making a purchase through your affiliate link.

Providing Personal Experience

One of the most powerful ways to make your product review persuasive is by sharing your personal experience with the product. If you have used the product yourself, provide an honest and detailed account of your experience. Discuss how the product has helped you and why you believe it can benefit your audience as well. Personal anecdotes and stories can make your review more relatable and trustworthy.

Including Pros and Cons

While it is important to highlight the benefits of the product, it is equally important to provide a balanced perspective by discussing the drawbacks or limitations. Including both the pros and cons of the product shows that you are providing an unbiased review and helps your audience make an informed decision. Be honest and transparent about any potential downsides, as this will build trust with your readers.

Using Persuasive Language

To make your product review more persuasive, use language that evokes emotion and creates a sense of urgency. Use powerful adjectives and descriptive phrases to paint a vivid picture of the product's benefits. Incorporate persuasive techniques such as scarcity, social proof, and fear of missing out (FOMO) to motivate your audience to take action. However, it is important to strike a balance and avoid using overly salesy or exaggerated language, as this can come across as insincere.

Structuring Your Review

A well-structured review is easier to read and understand. Start your review with a compelling introduction that grabs the reader's attention and clearly states the purpose of the review. Provide a brief overview of the product and its key features.

Then, dive into the details, discussing each feature in depth and explaining how it benefits the user. Use subheadings to break up the content and make it more scannable. Finally, conclude your review by summarizing the key points and reiterating your recommendation.

Incorporating Visuals

Visuals can greatly enhance the effectiveness of your product review. Include high-quality images or videos of the product to give your audience a visual representation of what they can expect. Screenshots, infographics, and comparison charts can also be used to illustrate the product's features and benefits. Visuals not only make your review more engaging but also help your audience visualize themselves using the product.

Adding Call-to-Action

To maximize your affiliate sales, it is crucial to include a clear and compelling call-to-action (CTA) in your product review. Encourage your readers to take the next step, whether it is clicking on your affiliate link, signing up for a free trial, or making a purchase. Use persuasive language and create a sense of urgency to motivate your audience to act immediately. Place your CTA strategically throughout your review, making it easily accessible and visible.

Honesty and Transparency

Above all, it is essential to maintain honesty and transparency in your product reviews. Your audience relies on your recommendations and trusts your opinion. If you promote a product solely for the sake of earning a commission, it will damage your credibility and reputation. Only promote products that you genuinely believe in and have personally vetted. Disclose your affiliate relationship and be transparent about any potential biases. By being honest and transparent, you will build trust with your audience and increase the likelihood of them making a purchase through your affiliate link.

Writing persuasive product reviews is a skill that can significantly impact your affiliate marketing success. By understanding the product, highlighting its benefits, providing personal experience, including pros and cons, using persuasive language, structuring your review effectively, incorporating visuals, adding a call-to-action, and maintaining honesty and transparency, you can create compelling product reviews that drive affiliate sales and help you achieve a six-figure income in affiliate marketing.

5.2 Crafting Engaging Blog Posts

Crafting engaging blog posts is an essential skill for any affiliate marketer looking to attract and retain a loyal audience. Blogging allows you to provide valuable content to your readers while subtly promoting your affiliate products or services. In this section, we will explore the key elements of creating compelling blog posts that drive traffic, engage readers, and ultimately lead to affiliate sales.

Understanding Your Target Audience

Before you start writing blog posts, it's crucial to have a deep understanding of your target audience. Knowing their needs, interests, and pain points will help you create content that resonates with them. Conduct thorough research to identify your audience's demographics, preferences, and online behavior. This information will guide your content creation process and ensure that your blog posts are relevant and valuable to your readers.

Choosing Relevant Topics

Once you have a clear understanding of your target audience, it's time to choose relevant topics for your blog posts. Look for subjects that align with your niche and address the needs and interests of your audience. Conduct keyword research to identify popular search terms related to your niche. This will help you optimize your blog posts for search engines and attract organic traffic.

Compelling Headlines

The headline of your blog post is the first thing that readers see, so it needs to be attention-grabbing and compelling. A well-crafted headline can entice readers to click on your blog post and read further. Use power words, numbers, and emotional triggers to make your headlines more captivating. Additionally, consider incorporating keywords into your headlines to improve search engine visibility.

Engaging Introductions

After capturing your readers' attention with a compelling headline, it's essential to hook them with an engaging introduction. Your introduction should provide a brief overview of what readers can expect from the blog post and why it's relevant to them. Consider starting with a thought-provoking question, a surprising statistic, or a relatable anecdote to captivate your audience from the start.

Valuable and Informative Content

The heart of your blog post lies in the content itself. To keep your readers engaged and coming back for more, it's crucial to provide valuable and informative content. Share your expertise, insights, and unique perspective on the topic at hand. Use examples, case studies, and data to support your claims and make your content more credible. Break up your content into easily digestible sections with subheadings, bullet points, and numbered lists to improve readability.

Visual Appeal

In addition to well-written content, incorporating visual elements into your blog posts can enhance their appeal. Use relevant and high-quality images, infographics, and videos to break up the text and make your blog posts more visually appealing. Visuals not only make your content more engaging but also help convey information more effectively. Ensure that your visuals are properly optimized for web use to avoid slowing down your website's loading speed.

Call-to-Action (CTA)

Every blog post should include a clear and compelling call-to-action (CTA) that encourages readers to take the desired action. Whether it's signing up for a newsletter, downloading a free resource, or making a purchase, your CTA should be persuasive and prominently displayed. Use action-oriented language and create a sense of urgency to motivate readers to act immediately.

SEO Optimization

To maximize the visibility of your blog posts and attract organic traffic, it's crucial to optimize them for search engines. Conduct keyword research and strategically incorporate relevant keywords into your blog posts. Use them naturally in your headings, subheadings, and throughout the content. Additionally, optimize your meta tags, URL structure, and image alt tags to improve your blog post's search engine ranking.

Consistency and Frequency

Consistency and frequency are key to building a loyal readership. Develop a content calendar and stick to a regular posting schedule. This will help you establish a routine and keep your audience engaged. Aim to provide fresh and valuable content consistently, whether it's weekly, bi-weekly, or monthly. Regularly engaging with your audience through blog posts will help you build trust and credibility over time.

Encouraging Engagement

Encouraging reader engagement is crucial for building a community around your blog. Include social sharing buttons to make it easy for readers to share your content on their preferred social media platforms. Respond to comments and engage with your readers to foster a sense of community and encourage further interaction. Consider ending your blog posts with a question or a call-to-action that prompts readers to leave comments and share their thoughts.

Crafting engaging blog posts is a continuous learning process. Pay attention to your analytics and track the performance of your blog posts. Analyze which topics and formats resonate the most with your audience and adjust your content strategy accordingly. By consistently providing valuable and engaging blog posts, you can attract a loyal audience, drive traffic to your affiliate offers, and ultimately achieve a six-figure income through affiliate marketing.

5.3 Producing Informative Video Content

Video content has become increasingly popular in recent years, and it has proven to be a highly effective medium for affiliate marketing. With the rise of platforms like YouTube and the widespread use of social media, producing informative video content can help you reach a wider audience and increase your affiliate sales. In this section, we will explore the strategies and techniques you can use to create compelling video content that drives traffic and generates conversions.

Why Video Content Matters in Affiliate Marketing

Video content offers several advantages over other forms of content when it comes to affiliate marketing. Here are a few reasons why you should consider incorporating video into your affiliate marketing strategy:

1. **Engagement:** Videos have the power to captivate and engage viewers in a way that text-based content cannot. By using visuals, audio, and storytelling techniques, you can create a more immersive and memorable experience for your audience.

2. **Demonstration:** Video allows you to demonstrate products or services in action, giving your audience a better understanding of their features and benefits. This can be particularly effective for promoting physical products or software.

3. **Trust and Authority:** Seeing a real person on video can help build trust and establish your authority in your niche. By providing valuable information and demonstrating your expertise, you can position yourself as a trusted source of recommendations and advice.

4. **Shareability:** Video content is highly shareable, especially on social media platforms. When your audience finds your videos valuable and informative, they are more likely to share them with their friends and followers, increasing your reach and potential for affiliate sales.

Creating Informative and Engaging Video Content

To produce informative video content that drives affiliate sales, consider the following strategies:

1. Identify Your Target Audience

Before creating any video content, it's crucial to understand your target audience. Research their demographics, interests, and pain points to tailor your videos to their specific needs. By addressing their concerns and providing solutions, you can establish a deeper connection and increase the likelihood of conversions.

There are various video formats you can choose from, depending on your niche and audience preferences. Some popular formats include:

- **Product Reviews:** Reviewing products or services in video format allows you to provide an in-depth analysis and showcase the benefits and features. Be honest and transparent in your reviews to maintain credibility.

- **Tutorials and How-To Guides:** Creating tutorials and how-to videos can be highly valuable for your audience. Teach them how to use a product or solve a problem, and include affiliate links in the video description or as overlays within the video.

- **Interviews and Expert Insights:** Conducting interviews with industry experts or influencers can provide valuable insights for your audience. This type of content can help establish your authority and credibility in your niche.

- **Behind-the-Scenes and Vlogs:** Sharing behind-the-scenes footage or vlogs can give your audience a glimpse into your life and business. This personal touch can help build a stronger connection with your viewers.

3. Plan and Script Your Videos

To ensure your videos are informative and engaging, it's essential to plan and script them in advance. Outline the key points you want to cover and create a structure for your video. This will help you stay focused and deliver your message effectively.

4. Use High-Quality Equipment and Editing Software

Investing in good-quality equipment, such as a camera, microphone, and lighting, can significantly improve the production value of your videos. Additionally, using professional editing software can help you create polished and visually appealing videos.

5. Optimize Your Videos for Search Engines

Just like written content, video content can be optimized for search engines. Conduct keyword research to identify relevant keywords and incorporate them into your video titles, descriptions, and tags. This will increase the visibility of your videos and attract organic traffic.

6. Include Calls to Action (CTAs)

Don't forget to include clear and compelling calls to action in your videos. Encourage viewers to take the desired action, such as clicking on affiliate links, subscribing to your channel, or visiting your website. CTAs help guide your audience towards the next step in the affiliate marketing process.

Once you've created your video content, it's essential to promote it to reach a wider audience. Share your videos on social media platforms, embed them in blog posts, and consider collaborating with other content creators in your niche. The more exposure your videos get, the higher the chances of driving traffic and generating affiliate sales.

Conclusion

Producing informative video content is a powerful strategy for affiliate marketers looking to increase their reach and generate conversions. By leveraging the engagement and shareability of video, you can establish trust, provide valuable information, and drive targeted traffic to your affiliate offers. Remember to identify your target audience, choose the right video format, plan and script your videos, optimize for search engines, include CTAs, and promote your videos to maximize their impact. With the right approach, video content can become a valuable asset in your affiliate marketing arsenal.

5.4 Creating Attention-Grabbing Social Media Posts

Social media has become an integral part of our daily lives, and it presents a massive opportunity for affiliate marketers to reach a wider audience and generate more sales. With billions of active users on platforms like Facebook, Instagram, Twitter, and LinkedIn, creating attention-grabbing social media posts can significantly boost your affiliate marketing efforts. In this section, we will explore effective strategies to create compelling social media posts that drive engagement and increase conversions.

Understanding the Power of Social Media

Social media platforms offer a unique opportunity to connect with your target audience on a personal level. By leveraging the power of social media, you can build a loyal following, establish yourself as an authority in your niche, and ultimately drive more traffic to your affiliate offers. However, it's important to approach social media marketing strategically and create content that resonates with your audience.

Know Your Target Audience

Before you start creating social media posts, it's crucial to understand your target audience. Who are they? What are their interests, pain points, and aspirations? By gaining a deep understanding of your audience, you can tailor your content to their needs and preferences. Conduct market research, analyze your competitors' social media presence, and engage with your audience to gather insights that will inform your content creation strategy.

Craft Compelling Headlines

The first step to grabbing attention on social media is to create compelling headlines. Your headline should be concise, attention-grabbing, and evoke curiosity. It should entice users to click on your post and learn more. Use power words, ask questions, or make bold statements to pique curiosity and encourage engagement. Remember, the headline is the first impression, so make it count.

Use Eye-Catching Visuals

Visual content is highly effective in capturing attention on social media. Incorporate eye-catching images, videos, infographics, or GIFs into your posts to make them stand out in users' feeds. Visuals should be relevant to your content and convey your message effectively. Use high-quality images, vibrant colors, and compelling visuals that align with your brand and resonate with your audience.

Keep it Short and Snappy

Social media users have short attention spans, so it's essential to keep your posts concise and to the point. Aim for bite-sized content that delivers value quickly. Use bullet points, subheadings, or emojis to break up text and make it more scannable. Focus on delivering a clear message and call to action in a concise manner.

Incorporate Storytelling

Storytelling is a powerful tool to engage your audience and create an emotional connection. Craft compelling stories that relate to your audience's pain points, desires, or aspirations. Use storytelling techniques to captivate your audience and make your content more memorable. Whether it's a personal anecdote, a customer success story, or a narrative that highlights the benefits of your affiliate product, storytelling can make your social media posts more relatable and persuasive.

Leverage User-Generated Content

User-generated content (UGC) is a valuable asset for affiliate marketers. Encourage your audience to share their experiences with your affiliate products and services. Repost positive reviews, testimonials, or user-generated images and videos to showcase social proof and build trust. UGC not only adds authenticity to your social media posts but also encourages engagement and drives conversions.

Use Hashtags Strategically

Hashtags are a powerful tool to increase the visibility of your social media posts. Research relevant hashtags that are popular in your niche and incorporate them into your content. Hashtags help categorize your posts and make them discoverable by users who are interested in similar topics. However, use hashtags sparingly and avoid overloading your posts with too many hashtags, as it can make your content appear spammy.

Social media is all about building relationships and engaging with your audience. Respond to comments, messages, and mentions promptly. Encourage discussions, ask questions, and seek feedback from your followers. Engaging with your audience not only strengthens your relationship with them but also increases the visibility of your posts and expands your reach.

Analyze and Optimize

To maximize the effectiveness of your social media posts, it's crucial to analyze their performance and make data-driven optimizations. Use social media analytics tools to track metrics such as reach, engagement, click-through rates, and conversions. Identify the types of posts that resonate the most with your audience and replicate their success. Experiment with different content formats, headlines, visuals, and calls to action to find the optimal combination that drives the highest engagement and conversions.

In conclusion, creating attention-grabbing social media posts is a crucial aspect of successful affiliate marketing. By understanding your target audience, crafting compelling headlines, using eye-catching visuals, incorporating storytelling, leveraging user-generated content, and engaging with your audience, you can create social media posts that drive engagement and increase conversions. Remember to analyze and optimize your posts based on data to continuously improve your social media marketing strategy.

Building an Email List for Affiliate Marketing

6.1 Understanding the Importance of Email Marketing

Email marketing is a crucial component of any successful affiliate marketing strategy. It allows you to build a direct line of communication with your audience, nurture relationships, and ultimately drive more sales. In this section, we will explore the importance of email marketing and how you can leverage it to maximize your affiliate income.

The Power of Email Marketing

Email marketing has consistently proven to be one of the most effective marketing channels for affiliate marketers. Here are some key reasons why it is so powerful:

1. **Direct Communication**: Email allows you to reach your audience directly in their inbox. Unlike social media or search engine algorithms, you have complete control over who receives your message and when.

2. **Personalization**: With email marketing, you can personalize your messages based on your subscribers' interests, preferences, and behaviors. This level of personalization helps you build stronger connections and increase engagement.

3. **Targeted Audience**: Your email list consists of people who have willingly opted in to receive updates from you. This means they are already interested in what you have to offer, making them highly targeted and more likely to convert into customers.

4. **Higher Conversion Rates**: Studies have consistently shown that email marketing has higher conversion rates compared to other marketing channels. This is because email allows you to deliver targeted and relevant content directly to your subscribers, increasing the chances of them taking action.

5. **Cost-Effective**: Email marketing is a cost-effective way to promote your affiliate products. Unlike paid advertising, which can quickly eat up your budget, email marketing allows you to reach a large audience without significant expenses.

Building an Email List

To leverage the power of email marketing, you need to build a quality email list. Here are some strategies to help you grow your list:

1. **Lead Magnets**: Offer valuable incentives, such as ebooks, guides, or exclusive content, in exchange for your visitors' email addresses. These lead magnets should be relevant to your niche and provide real value to your audience.

2. **Opt-In Forms**: Place opt-in forms strategically on your website to capture email addresses. Consider using pop-ups, slide-ins, or embedded forms in high-visibility areas to maximize conversions.

3. **Content Upgrades**: Create additional resources or bonus content that complements your blog posts or videos. Offer these upgrades in exchange for email sign-ups to provide extra value to your audience.

4. **Social Media Promotion**: Leverage your social media platforms to promote your lead magnets and encourage people to join your email list. Use compelling copy and visuals to entice your followers to take action.

5. **Guest Blogging**: Write guest posts for popular blogs in your niche and include a call-to-action within your author bio or within the content itself. Direct readers to a landing page where they can sign up for your email list.

Setting Up Email Marketing Campaigns

Once you have built your email list, it's time to set up effective email marketing campaigns. Here are some steps to get you started:

1. **Choose an Email Service Provider (ESP)**: Select a reputable ESP that offers the features and functionality you need. Popular options include Mailchimp, ConvertKit, and AWeber.

2. **Segment Your List**: Divide your email list into segments based on demographics, interests, or engagement levels. This allows you to send targeted and relevant content to specific groups, increasing the effectiveness of your campaigns.

3. **Create Engaging Content**: Craft compelling email content that resonates with your audience. Use a mix of informative and promotional emails to keep your subscribers engaged and interested in what you have to offer.

4. **Automate Your Campaigns**: Set up automated email sequences to nurture your subscribers and guide them through the buyer's journey. These sequences can include welcome emails, educational content, and promotional offers.

5. **Monitor and Analyze**: Regularly monitor the performance of your email campaigns. Pay attention to open rates, click-through rates, and conversion rates to identify areas for improvement and optimize your campaigns.

Nurturing and Engaging Subscribers

Building a strong relationship with your email subscribers is crucial for long-term success in affiliate marketing. Here are some tips to nurture and engage your subscribers:

1. **Provide Value**: Focus on delivering valuable content that educates, entertains, or solves a problem for your subscribers. Avoid being overly promotional and prioritize building trust and credibility.

2. **Personalize Your Emails**: Use personalization tags to address your subscribers by their names and tailor your content based on their preferences. This helps create a more personalized experience and strengthens the connection with your audience.

3. **Engage with Your Subscribers**: Encourage your subscribers to interact with your emails by asking questions, conducting surveys, or hosting contests. This not only increases engagement but also provides valuable insights into your audience's preferences and needs.

4. **Offer Exclusive Benefits**: Provide exclusive discounts, early access to promotions, or special bonuses to your email subscribers. This makes them feel valued and incentivizes them to stay subscribed and continue engaging with your content.

5. **Maintain Consistency**: Establish a consistent email schedule to keep your subscribers engaged. Whether it's a weekly newsletter or a monthly roundup, consistency helps build anticipation and keeps your brand top of mind.

Remember, email marketing is a long-term strategy that requires consistent effort and nurturing. By building a quality email list and implementing effective email marketing campaigns, you can significantly boost your affiliate income and achieve your six-figure income goals.

6.2 Creating Lead Magnets

In the world of affiliate marketing, building an email list is crucial for long-term success. An email list allows you to connect with your audience on a more personal level, nurture relationships, and promote affiliate products effectively. However, simply asking people to join your email list may not be enough to entice them. This is where lead magnets come into play.

Lead magnets are valuable resources or incentives that you offer to your website visitors in exchange for their email addresses. They are designed to attract and capture the attention of your target audience, providing them with something of value that solves a specific problem or fulfills a need. By offering a lead magnet, you can entice visitors to willingly provide their email addresses, allowing you to build a targeted and engaged email list.

Creating effective lead magnets requires careful planning and consideration. Here are some steps to help you create compelling lead magnets that will attract your target audience and grow your email list:

1. Understand Your Target Audience

Before you can create a lead magnet, it's essential to have a deep understanding of your target audience. What are their pain points, challenges, and desires? What kind of information or resources would they find valuable? Conduct market research, analyze your audience's demographics and interests, and gather insights from your existing audience to gain a clear understanding of their needs and preferences.

2. Identify a Specific Problem to Solve

Once you understand your target audience, identify a specific problem or challenge that they face. Your lead magnet should provide a solution or valuable information related to this problem. By addressing a specific pain point, you can position yourself as an expert and build trust with your audience.

3. Choose the Right Format

Lead magnets can come in various formats, such as ebooks, checklists, templates, video tutorials, webinars, or exclusive access to a membership site. Consider the preferences of your target audience and choose a format that aligns with their needs and preferences. For example, if your audience prefers visual content, a video tutorial or infographic might be more effective than a lengthy ebook.

4. Create High-Quality Content

The content of your lead magnet should be valuable, well-researched, and well-presented. Take the time to create high-quality content that provides actionable insights, practical tips, or step-by-step guidance. Ensure that the information you provide is accurate, up-to-date, and relevant to your audience's needs.

5. Design an Eye-Catching Cover or Landing Page

The visual appeal of your lead magnet is crucial in capturing the attention of your audience. Design an eye-catching cover or landing page that reflects the value and quality of your content. Use compelling headlines, attractive images, and clear calls-to-action to encourage visitors to download or access your lead magnet.

6. Optimize for Conversion

To maximize the effectiveness of your lead magnet, optimize it for conversion. This includes placing opt-in forms strategically on your website, using persuasive copywriting techniques, and offering a clear and compelling call-to-action. Make it easy for visitors to sign up for your email list and receive the lead magnet.

7. Promote Your Lead Magnet

Creating a lead magnet is only the first step. You also need to promote it to attract visitors and encourage them to opt-in. Utilize various marketing channels such as your website, blog, social media platforms, and email newsletters to promote your lead magnet. Consider running targeted advertising campaigns or collaborating with influencers in your niche to reach a wider audience.

8. Test and Refine

Once your lead magnet is live, track its performance and gather feedback from your audience. Monitor the conversion rates, engagement levels, and feedback to identify areas for improvement. Test different formats, headlines, or calls-to-action to optimize your lead magnet's effectiveness over time.

Remember, the success of your lead magnet depends on its relevance, value, and appeal to your target audience. Continuously analyze and refine your lead magnet strategy to ensure that it aligns with your audience's evolving needs and preferences. By creating compelling lead magnets, you can attract a highly engaged email list that will ultimately contribute to your affiliate marketing success.

6.3 Setting Up Email Marketing Campaigns

Email marketing is a powerful tool that can significantly boost your affiliate marketing efforts and help you generate a six-figure income. By building an email list of engaged subscribers, you can establish a direct line of communication with your audience and promote affiliate products effectively. In this section, we will explore the steps to set up successful email marketing campaigns that drive conversions and maximize your affiliate sales.

The Importance of Email Marketing

Email marketing is a crucial component of any successful affiliate marketing strategy. It allows you to build a relationship with your audience, nurture leads, and promote affiliate products directly to interested individuals. Here are some key reasons why email marketing is essential for your affiliate business:

1. **Direct communication**: Email provides a direct and personal way to connect with your audience. By sending targeted messages to your subscribers' inboxes, you can engage with them on a one-on-one level, increasing the chances of conversions.

2. **Higher conversion rates**: Studies have shown that email marketing consistently delivers higher conversion rates compared to other marketing channels. When done right, email campaigns can drive significant affiliate sales and generate a substantial income.

3. **Building trust and credibility**: By consistently delivering valuable content and recommendations to your subscribers, you can establish yourself as an authority in your niche. This builds trust and credibility, making your audience more likely to purchase products you recommend.

4. **Automation and scalability**: Email marketing platforms offer automation features that allow you to set up automated email sequences, saving you time and effort. Additionally, email marketing campaigns can be scaled easily as your subscriber list grows.

Creating Effective Email Marketing Campaigns

To set up successful email marketing campaigns for your affiliate business, follow these steps:

Step 1: Choose an Email Marketing Service Provider

Start by selecting a reliable email marketing service provider that suits your needs. Popular options include Mailchimp, AWeber, ConvertKit, and GetResponse. Consider factors such as pricing, ease of use, automation capabilities, and integration with other tools you use.

Step 2: Build Your Email List

The success of your email marketing campaigns depends on the quality and size of your email list. Implement strategies to attract subscribers, such as offering lead magnets, creating engaging content, and optimizing your website for conversions. Ensure that you comply with email marketing regulations, such as obtaining explicit consent from subscribers and providing an easy way to unsubscribe.

Segmenting your email list allows you to send targeted messages to specific groups of subscribers based on their interests, preferences, or behavior. This personalization increases the relevance of your emails and improves engagement and conversion rates. Common segmentation criteria include demographics, purchase history, engagement level, and interests.

Step 4: Create Compelling Email Content

Craft engaging and persuasive email content that resonates with your audience. Consider the following tips:

- **Subject lines**: Write attention-grabbing subject lines that entice subscribers to open your emails. Use personalization, urgency, curiosity, or offers to increase open rates.

- **Content structure**: Keep your emails concise and scannable. Use short paragraphs, bullet points, and subheadings to make your content easy to read. Include a clear call-to-action (CTA) that directs subscribers to take the desired action.

- **Value-driven content**: Provide valuable information, tips, or insights related to your niche. Share success stories, case studies, or product reviews that demonstrate the benefits of the affiliate products you promote.

- **Visuals**: Incorporate relevant images, videos, or infographics to make your emails visually appealing and engaging. Visual content can help convey your message more effectively and increase click-through rates.

Step 5: Automate Email Sequences

Set up automated email sequences to nurture and engage your subscribers. These sequences can include welcome emails, educational content, promotional offers, and follow-up messages. Use automation features provided by your email marketing service provider to schedule and trigger emails based on specific actions or time intervals.

Step 6: Monitor and Optimize Campaign Performance

Regularly monitor the performance of your email marketing campaigns to identify areas for improvement. Track metrics such as open rates, click-through rates, conversion rates, and unsubscribe rates. Use this data to optimize your campaigns by testing different subject lines, content formats, CTAs, and sending frequencies.

Step 7: Comply with Email Marketing Regulations

Ensure that your email marketing campaigns comply with relevant regulations, such as the CAN-SPAM Act in the United States or the General Data Protection Regulation (GDPR) in the European Union. Familiarize yourself with the requirements, such as including a physical mailing address, providing an unsubscribe option, and honoring subscriber preferences.

By following these steps and consistently delivering valuable content to your subscribers, you can set up effective email marketing campaigns that drive affiliate sales and help you achieve a six-figure income.

Remember, building a successful email list takes time and effort. Focus on providing value, nurturing relationships, and promoting relevant affiliate products to maximize your conversions and income.

6.4 Nurturing and Engaging Subscribers

Once you have successfully built an email list for your affiliate marketing business, the next step is to nurture and engage your subscribers. Nurturing your subscribers involves building a relationship with them, providing them with valuable content, and gaining their trust. Engaging your subscribers means keeping them interested and active, encouraging them to take action, and ultimately increasing your affiliate sales. In this section, we will explore effective strategies for nurturing and engaging your subscribers to maximize your affiliate marketing success.

6.4.1 Provide Valuable Content

One of the most important aspects of nurturing your subscribers is consistently providing them with valuable content. Your subscribers have willingly given you their email addresses because they believe you can offer them something of value. It is crucial to deliver on that promise by sending them high-quality content that is relevant to their interests and needs.

Consider creating a content calendar to plan and organize your email campaigns. This will help you stay consistent and ensure that you are providing a variety of content types to keep your subscribers engaged. Some content ideas include:

- Educational articles or blog posts: Share informative content that helps your subscribers solve a problem or learn something new related to your niche.
- Product reviews and recommendations: Provide honest and unbiased reviews of products or services that you have personally used and found beneficial. Include affiliate links within these reviews to generate sales.
- How-to guides and tutorials: Create step-by-step guides or video tutorials that teach your subscribers how to achieve a specific goal or complete a task related to your niche.
- Exclusive offers and discounts: Reward your subscribers by offering exclusive discounts or promotions on products or services that you promote as an affiliate.

Remember to always focus on providing value to your subscribers rather than solely promoting affiliate products. By consistently delivering valuable content, you will build trust and credibility with your audience, increasing the likelihood of them making purchases through your affiliate links.

6.4.2 Personalize Your Emails

Personalization is key to engaging your subscribers and making them feel valued. Instead of sending generic emails to your entire list, segment your subscribers based on their interests, preferences, or behavior. This allows you to tailor your emails to specific groups, increasing the relevance and effectiveness of your messages.

Consider using an email marketing platform that offers segmentation features. This will enable you to create targeted email campaigns based on various criteria such as demographics, past purchases, or engagement levels. By personalizing your emails, you can deliver content that resonates with each segment, leading to higher open rates, click-through rates, and conversions.

In addition to segmentation, addressing your subscribers by their names in your emails can also make a significant impact. It adds a personal touch and makes your emails feel more individualized. Most email marketing platforms allow you to easily insert personalized fields, such as the subscriber's first name, into your email templates.

6.4.3 Engage with Interactive Content

To keep your subscribers engaged and interested, consider incorporating interactive content into your email campaigns. Interactive content encourages subscribers to actively participate and interact with your emails, increasing their level of engagement and the likelihood of them taking action.

Some examples of interactive content you can include in your emails are:

- Quizzes or surveys: Create interactive quizzes or surveys that allow your subscribers to provide feedback or answer questions related to your niche. This not only engages them but also provides you with valuable insights and data.
- Polls or voting: Ask your subscribers to vote on a particular topic or share their opinions through polls. This can help you understand their preferences and tailor your content accordingly.
- Contests or giveaways: Organize contests or giveaways exclusively for your subscribers. Encourage them to participate by taking specific actions such as sharing your content, referring friends, or making a purchase through your affiliate links.

By incorporating interactive content, you can make your emails more engaging and interactive, increasing the chances of your subscribers taking the desired actions, such as clicking on affiliate links or making purchases.

Email automation is a powerful tool that allows you to send targeted and timely emails to your subscribers based on their behavior or predefined triggers. By setting up automated email sequences, you can nurture your subscribers without having to manually send individual emails for each interaction.

Consider implementing the following automated email sequences:

- Welcome series: When a new subscriber joins your email list, send them a series of welcome emails introducing yourself, providing valuable content, and guiding them through your affiliate offers.
- Abandoned cart recovery: If a subscriber adds products to their cart but doesn't complete the purchase, send them automated emails reminding them of the items and offering incentives to complete the purchase through your affiliate links.
- Upsell or cross-sell sequences: If a subscriber makes a purchase through your affiliate link, set up automated emails recommending complementary products or upgrades that they might be interested in.

By utilizing email automation, you can deliver targeted and relevant content to your subscribers at the right time, increasing engagement and ultimately driving more affiliate sales.

Engaging with your subscribers should not be a one-way street. Encourage two-way communication by actively seeking feedback, responding to their inquiries, and fostering a sense of community.

Consider implementing the following strategies to encourage two-way communication:

- Encourage replies: In your emails, explicitly invite your subscribers to reply with their thoughts, questions, or feedback. Respond to their emails promptly and personally to show that you value their input.
- Conduct surveys or polls: Regularly ask your subscribers for their opinions or suggestions through surveys or polls. This not only engages them but also provides you with valuable insights for improving your content or affiliate offers.
- Create a community: Consider creating a private Facebook group or forum where your subscribers can connect with each other, ask questions, and share their experiences. Actively participate in the community to foster engagement and build relationships with your subscribers.

By encouraging two-way communication, you create a more interactive and engaging experience for your subscribers, strengthening their connection with your brand and increasing their loyalty.

In conclusion, nurturing and engaging your subscribers is crucial for maximizing your affiliate marketing success. By providing valuable content, personalizing your emails, incorporating interactive content, utilizing email automation, and encouraging two-way communication, you can build strong relationships with your subscribers, increase their engagement, and ultimately drive more affiliate sales. Remember, the key is to consistently deliver value and foster a sense of trust and community with your subscribers.

Maximizing Affiliate Sales with Sales Funnels

7.1 Understanding Sales Funnels

In the world of affiliate marketing, understanding sales funnels is crucial to maximizing your affiliate sales and ultimately achieving a six-figure income. A sales funnel is a strategic process that guides potential customers through a series of steps, with the ultimate goal of converting them into paying customers. By implementing effective sales funnels, you can optimize your affiliate marketing efforts and significantly increase your earning potential.

What is a Sales Funnel?

A sales funnel is a visual representation of the customer journey, from the initial awareness stage to the final purchase. It consists of a series of steps or stages that potential customers go through, with each stage designed to move them closer to making a purchase. The primary purpose of a sales funnel is to nurture leads and guide them towards becoming paying customers.

The Stages of a Sales Funnel

A typical sales funnel consists of several stages, each serving a specific purpose in the customer journey. Let's take a closer look at each stage:

1. **Awareness**: This is the first stage of the sales funnel, where potential customers become aware of your product or service. At this stage, your goal is to attract their attention and generate interest in what you have to offer. This can be done through various marketing channels such as social media, content marketing, or paid advertising.

2. **Interest**: Once potential customers are aware of your product or service, the next stage is to capture their interest. This is where you provide them with valuable information, such as educational content or product demonstrations, to further engage them and build trust. The goal is to keep them interested and motivated to learn more.

3. **Decision**: In the decision stage, potential customers are evaluating their options and deciding whether to make a purchase. This is where you need to provide them with compelling reasons to choose your affiliate product over

your competitors. This can be done through persuasive product reviews, testimonials, or limited-time offers.

4. **Action**: The final stage of the sales funnel is the action stage, where potential customers make a purchase. At this point, they have gone through the awareness, interest, and decision stages and are ready to take action. Your goal is to make the purchasing process as seamless and convenient as possible, ensuring a smooth transition from potential customer to paying customer.

The Importance of Sales Funnels in Affiliate Marketing

Implementing sales funnels in your affiliate marketing strategy can have a significant impact on your earning potential. Here are a few reasons why sales funnels are crucial in affiliate marketing:

1. **Increased Conversion Rates**: By guiding potential customers through a series of steps, sales funnels help increase conversion rates. By providing valuable information, building trust, and addressing potential objections, you can significantly improve the chances of converting leads into paying customers.

2. **Targeted Marketing**: Sales funnels allow you to segment your audience and tailor your marketing messages accordingly. By understanding where potential customers are in the sales funnel, you can deliver personalized content and offers that resonate with their specific needs and interests. This targeted approach can lead to higher engagement and conversion rates.

3. **Maximized Revenue**: Sales funnels enable you to maximize your revenue by implementing upsells and cross-sells. Once a customer has made a purchase, you can offer them additional products or services that complement their initial purchase. This not only increases the average order value but also enhances the overall customer experience.

4. **Customer Retention**: Sales funnels are not just about acquiring new customers; they also play a crucial role in customer retention. By nurturing your existing customers and providing them with ongoing value, you can encourage repeat purchases and foster long-term relationships. This can lead to a steady stream of recurring revenue and increased customer loyalty.

Creating Effective Sales Funnels for Affiliate Marketing

To create effective sales funnels for your affiliate marketing business, consider the following tips:

1. **Understand Your Target Audience**: Before creating a sales funnel, it's essential to have a deep understanding of your target audience. Research their needs, pain points, and motivations to create content and offers that resonate with them.

2. **Map Out the Customer Journey**: Visualize the customer journey from the awareness stage to the final purchase. Identify the key touchpoints and create content and offers that align with each stage of the funnel.

3. **Provide Valuable Content**: At each stage of the funnel, provide valuable content that educates, informs, and builds trust with your audience. This can include blog posts, videos, case studies, or free resources that address their specific needs and challenges.

4. **Optimize Conversion Points**: Identify the critical conversion points in your sales funnel and optimize them for maximum conversions. This can include optimizing landing pages, call-to-action buttons, and checkout processes to reduce friction and improve the user experience.

5. **Implement Upsells and Cross-Sells**: Once a customer has made a purchase, offer them additional products or services that complement their initial purchase. This can significantly increase your revenue per customer and enhance the overall customer experience.

6. **Track and Analyze Performance**: Regularly track and analyze the performance of your sales funnels to identify areas for improvement. Use analytics tools to measure conversion rates, customer behavior, and revenue generated to make data-driven decisions.

By understanding and implementing sales funnels in your affiliate marketing strategy, you can optimize your efforts, increase your conversion rates, and ultimately achieve a six-figure income. Remember, creating effective sales funnels takes time and experimentation, so be prepared to test and refine your approach to find what works best for your audience and niche.

7.2 Creating Landing Pages

A landing page is a crucial component of any successful affiliate marketing campaign. It is a standalone web page that is specifically designed to convert visitors into leads or customers. Creating effective landing pages is essential for maximizing your affiliate sales and achieving a six-figure income per month. In this section, we will explore the key elements and strategies for creating high-converting landing pages.

The Purpose of a Landing Page

The primary purpose of a landing page is to capture the attention of your target audience and persuade them to take a specific action, such as making a purchase or signing up for a newsletter. Unlike a regular website page, a landing page is focused on a single objective and eliminates distractions that may divert visitors' attention away from the desired action.

Key Elements of a Landing Page

To create a high-converting landing page, you need to consider the following key elements:

1. Compelling Headline

The headline is the first thing visitors see when they land on your page. It should be attention-grabbing, concise, and clearly communicate the value proposition of your offer. A compelling headline can significantly impact the conversion rate of your landing page.

2. Clear and Concise Copy

The copy on your landing page should be clear, concise, and persuasive. It should highlight the benefits of your offer and address any objections or concerns that your audience may have. Use bullet points, subheadings, and short paragraphs to make the content easily scannable.

3. Engaging Visuals

Including relevant and visually appealing images or videos can enhance the overall user experience and make your landing page more engaging. Visuals can help convey your message more effectively and increase the chances of conversion.

4. Call-to-Action (CTA)

A strong and prominent call-to-action is crucial for guiding visitors towards the desired action. The CTA should be clear, compelling, and prominently displayed on the page. Use action-oriented language and consider using contrasting colors to make the CTA button stand out.

5. Trust Indicators

Building trust with your audience is essential for increasing conversions. Include trust indicators such as customer testimonials, reviews, trust badges, and security seals to instill confidence in your visitors and alleviate any concerns they may have.

6. Mobile Optimization

With the increasing use of mobile devices, it is crucial to ensure that your landing page is optimized for mobile viewing. Make sure the page is responsive and loads quickly on mobile devices to provide a seamless user experience.

Strategies for Creating High-Converting Landing Pages

Now that you understand the key elements of a landing page, let's explore some strategies to create high-converting landing pages:

1. Keep it Simple

Simplicity is key when it comes to landing pages. Avoid cluttering the page with unnecessary elements or excessive information. Keep the design clean and focused on the main objective. A simple and intuitive layout will help visitors navigate the page easily and increase the chances of conversion.

2. Use Persuasive Copywriting Techniques

Effective copywriting is crucial for persuading visitors to take action. Use persuasive techniques such as storytelling, addressing pain points, highlighting benefits, and creating a sense of urgency. Craft compelling headlines and use persuasive language throughout the copy to engage your audience and drive conversions.

3. A/B Testing

A/B testing is a powerful technique for optimizing your landing pages. Create multiple versions of your landing page and test different elements such as headlines, copy, visuals, and CTAs. Analyze the performance of each version and make data-driven decisions to improve conversion rates.

4. Implement Conversion Tracking

To measure the effectiveness of your landing pages, it is essential to implement conversion tracking. Use tools like Google Analytics or other tracking software to monitor key metrics such as conversion rate, bounce rate, and average time on page. This data will help you identify areas for improvement and optimize your landing pages for better results.

5. Continuously Optimize

Creating high-converting landing pages is an ongoing process. Continuously monitor the performance of your landing pages and make iterative improvements based on data and user feedback. Test different elements, analyze the results, and make adjustments to maximize conversions.

Conclusion

Creating effective landing pages is a critical aspect of maximizing your affiliate sales and achieving a six-figure income per month. By understanding the key elements and implementing proven strategies, you can create landing pages that engage your audience, drive conversions, and ultimately lead to significant affiliate marketing success. Remember to keep your landing pages simple, use persuasive copywriting techniques, and continuously optimize based on data and user feedback.

7.3 Designing Effective Sales Pages

In affiliate marketing, the success of your sales funnel heavily relies on the design and effectiveness of your sales pages. A well-designed sales page can significantly increase your conversion rates and ultimately lead to higher affiliate sales. In this section, we will explore the key elements and strategies for designing effective sales pages that drive results.

Understanding the Purpose of a Sales Page

Before diving into the design process, it's crucial to understand the purpose of a sales page. A sales page is a dedicated landing page that aims to persuade visitors to take a specific action, such as making a purchase or signing up for a service. Its primary goal is to convert visitors into customers by showcasing the value and benefits of the product or service you are promoting.

Key Elements of an Effective Sales Page

To design an effective sales page, you need to incorporate the following key elements:

1. Attention-Grabbing Headline

The headline is the first thing visitors see when they land on your sales page. It should be compelling, attention-grabbing, and clearly communicate the main benefit or solution your product offers. A strong headline can captivate your audience and encourage them to continue reading.

2. Engaging Sales Copy

The sales copy is the heart of your sales page. It should be persuasive, informative, and highlight the unique selling points of the product or service. Use persuasive language, storytelling techniques, and customer testimonials to build trust and credibility. Focus on addressing the pain points of your target audience and how your product can solve their problems.

3. Clear Call-to-Action (CTA)

A clear and prominent call-to-action is essential for guiding visitors towards the desired action. Use a visually appealing button or link that stands out from the rest of the page. Clearly state the action you want visitors to take, such as "Buy Now," "Sign Up," or "Learn More." Make sure the CTA is easily accessible and strategically placed on the page.

4. Visuals and Multimedia

Incorporating relevant visuals and multimedia elements can enhance the overall appeal and engagement of your sales page. Use high-quality product images, videos, infographics, or interactive elements to showcase the features and benefits of the product. Visuals can help break up the text and make the page more visually appealing and engaging.

5. Social Proof

Including social proof, such as customer testimonials, reviews, or case studies, can significantly boost the credibility and trustworthiness of your sales page. Positive feedback from satisfied customers can help alleviate any doubts or concerns potential buyers may have. Consider including real-life examples and success stories to demonstrate the effectiveness of the product.

6. Benefits and Features

Clearly outline the key benefits and features of the product or service you are promoting. Highlight how it can solve specific problems or improve the lives of your target audience. Use bullet points or short paragraphs to make the information easily scannable and digestible.

7. Limited-Time Offers or Scarcity

Creating a sense of urgency or scarcity can motivate visitors to take immediate action. Offer limited-time discounts, bonuses, or exclusive deals to create a fear of missing out (FOMO). Clearly communicate the urgency and scarcity of the offer to encourage visitors to make a purchase decision quickly.

8. Mobile-Friendly Design

With the increasing use of mobile devices, it's crucial to ensure that your sales page is mobile-friendly. Optimize the design and layout to provide a seamless user experience across different screen sizes. Test your sales page on various devices to ensure it loads quickly and displays correctly.

Design Tips for Effective Sales Pages

In addition to the key elements mentioned above, here are some design tips to create effective sales pages:

1. Keep it Clean and Simple

Avoid cluttering your sales page with excessive text, images, or distractions. Keep the design clean, simple, and focused on the main message and call-to-action. Use ample white space to make the content more readable and visually appealing.

2. Use Visual Hierarchy

Guide visitors' attention by using visual hierarchy techniques. Use larger fonts, bold text, or color contrast to emphasize important points or key benefits. Arrange the content in a logical and easy-to-follow order to guide visitors through the sales page.

3. Use High-Quality Images

Choose high-quality images that are relevant to the product or service you are promoting. Use images that evoke emotions or demonstrate the desired outcome of using the product. Avoid using generic stock photos and opt for authentic and relatable visuals.

Designing an effective sales page is an iterative process. Continuously test different elements, layouts, and variations to optimize your conversion rates. Use A/B testing to compare different versions of your sales page and identify what resonates best with your audience.

Include trust symbols, such as security badges, certifications, or partner logos, to enhance the credibility of your sales page. These symbols can help alleviate any concerns visitors may have about the legitimacy or safety of the transaction.

Conclusion

Designing effective sales pages is a crucial aspect of maximizing your affiliate sales. By incorporating attention-grabbing headlines, engaging sales copy, clear CTAs, visuals, social proof, and other key elements, you can create persuasive and high-converting sales pages. Remember to continuously test and optimize your sales pages to improve your conversion rates and drive more affiliate sales.

7.4 Implementing Upsells and Cross-Sells

Once you have successfully attracted visitors to your website and converted them into customers, it's time to maximize your affiliate sales by implementing upsells and cross-sells. Upselling and cross-selling are powerful strategies that can significantly increase your revenue without requiring additional marketing efforts. In this section, we will explore how you can effectively implement upsells and cross-sells in your affiliate marketing business.

Understanding Upsells and Cross-Sells

Before diving into the implementation process, let's clarify the difference between upsells and cross-sells. Upselling involves offering a higher-priced product or service to a customer who has already made a purchase. The goal is to encourage the customer to upgrade their purchase and spend more money. For example, if a customer buys a basic fitness program, you can offer them an advanced program with additional features and benefits at a higher price.

On the other hand, cross-selling involves offering complementary or related products to a customer who has already made a purchase. The goal is to increase the average order value by suggesting additional products that enhance the customer's experience. For example, if a customer buys a camera, you can offer them a memory card, camera bag, and tripod as cross-sell options.

To effectively implement upsells and cross-sells, you need to identify the right opportunities within your affiliate marketing business. Here are a few strategies to help you identify upsell and cross-sell opportunities:

1. **Analyze your product offerings**: Take a close look at your affiliate products and identify which ones have higher-priced or complementary alternatives. These products can serve as potential upsell and cross-sell options.

2. **Understand your target audience**: Gain a deep understanding of your target audience's needs and preferences. This will help you identify products or services that align with their interests and can be offered as upsells or cross-sells.

3. **Leverage customer data**: Analyze your customer data to identify patterns and trends. Look for common purchasing behaviors and preferences that can guide your upsell and cross-sell strategies.

4. **Research affiliate programs**: Explore different affiliate programs and networks to find products or services that complement your existing offerings. Look for programs that offer upsell and cross-sell options to maximize your revenue potential.

Implementing Upsells

Now that you have identified potential upsell opportunities, it's time to implement them effectively. Here are some strategies to help you implement upsells in your affiliate marketing business:

1. **Create compelling upsell offers**: Develop attractive offers that clearly communicate the additional value and benefits of the upsell product. Highlight how the upsell can enhance the customer's experience or solve a specific problem they may have.

2. **Position upsells strategically**: Place your upsell offers at strategic points in the customer journey. For example, you can present the upsell offer immediately after the customer completes their initial purchase or during the checkout process.

3. **Offer tiered pricing**: Provide multiple upsell options at different price points to cater to different customer preferences. This allows customers to choose the upsell that best suits their needs and budget.

4. **Bundle products**: Create product bundles that combine the initial purchase with an upsell product. This not only increases the perceived value but also encourages customers to upgrade their purchase.

5. **Provide incentives**: Offer incentives such as discounts, bonuses, or exclusive access to encourage customers to take advantage of the upsell offer. Limited-time offers or scarcity tactics can create a sense of urgency and drive conversions.

Implementing cross-sells requires a slightly different approach. Here are some strategies to effectively implement cross-sells in your affiliate marketing business:

1. **Recommend relevant products**: Analyze the customer's initial purchase and recommend related products that enhance their experience or provide additional value. Ensure that the cross-sell products are genuinely relevant and beneficial to the customer.

2. **Display cross-sell options prominently**: Place cross-sell options in strategic locations on your website, such as product pages, shopping carts, or checkout pages. Make sure they are visually appealing and clearly communicate the benefits of the cross-sell products.

3. **Use personalized recommendations**: Leverage customer data and browsing history to provide personalized cross-sell recommendations. This can significantly increase the chances of conversion as customers feel that the recommendations are tailored to their specific needs.

4. **Offer discounts or incentives**: Provide discounts or incentives for customers who add cross-sell products to their cart. This can motivate them to make additional purchases and increase the average order value.

5. **Use social proof**: Incorporate customer reviews, testimonials, or ratings for the cross-sell products to build trust and credibility. Social proof can help alleviate any concerns or doubts customers may have about the additional purchase.

To ensure the effectiveness of your upsell and cross-sell strategies, it's crucial to monitor and optimize their performance. Here are some tips to help you monitor and optimize your upsells and cross-sells:

1. **Track conversion rates**: Monitor the conversion rates of your upsell and cross-sell offers to identify which ones are performing well and which ones need improvement. Use analytics tools to track the success of your offers and make data-driven decisions.

2. **A/B test your offers**: Conduct A/B tests to compare different upsell and cross-sell offers. Test different pricing, messaging, and positioning to determine which variations yield the highest conversion rates.

3. **Collect customer feedback**: Gather feedback from customers who have taken advantage of your upsell and cross-sell offers. This feedback can provide valuable insights into the effectiveness of your strategies and help you make necessary improvements.

4. **Continuously optimize**: Regularly review and optimize your upsell and cross-sell strategies based on the data and feedback you collect. Experiment with different offers, placements, and incentives to find the most effective combinations.

By implementing upsells and cross-sells in your affiliate marketing business, you can significantly increase your revenue and maximize the value you provide to your customers. Remember to identify the right opportunities, create compelling offers, and continuously monitor and optimize your strategies to achieve the best results.

Optimizing Affiliate Marketing for Mobile Devices

8.1 The Importance of Mobile Optimization

In today's digital age, mobile devices have become an integral part of our lives. People are increasingly using their smartphones and tablets to browse the internet, shop online, and interact with content. As an affiliate marketer, it is crucial to recognize the importance of mobile optimization in order to maximize your earning potential.

Mobile optimization refers to the process of ensuring that your website and marketing materials are designed and formatted to provide an optimal user experience on mobile devices. This includes making your website responsive, optimizing loading times, and adapting your content to fit smaller screens.

The rise of mobile usage has had a significant impact on the affiliate marketing industry. According to recent studies, mobile devices account for more than half of all internet traffic worldwide. This means that if your website is not mobile-friendly, you are potentially missing out on a large portion of your target audience.

One of the key reasons why mobile optimization is crucial for affiliate marketers is the impact it has on search engine rankings. Search engines like Google prioritize mobile-friendly websites in their search results, as they want to provide the best user experience for their mobile users. If your website is not optimized for mobile, it is likely to rank lower in search results, resulting in less organic traffic and fewer potential customers.

Furthermore, mobile optimization plays a vital role in improving user engagement and conversion rates. Studies have shown that mobile users are more likely to abandon a website if it takes too long to load or if the layout is difficult to navigate. By optimizing your website for mobile, you can provide a seamless and user-friendly experience, increasing the chances of visitors staying on your site and taking the desired action, such as making a purchase or signing up for a newsletter.

Another important aspect of mobile optimization is the increasing popularity of mobile commerce, also known as m-commerce. With the convenience of mobile devices, more and more people are using their smartphones and tablets to make online purchases. As an affiliate marketer, this presents a significant opportunity to generate revenue. By ensuring that your website is mobile-friendly and optimized for m-commerce, you can tap into this growing market and increase your chances of earning a six-figure income.

In addition to website optimization, mobile advertising strategies are also crucial for affiliate marketers. Mobile advertising allows you to reach your target audience directly on their mobile devices through various channels such as mobile apps, social media platforms, and mobile search ads. By leveraging mobile advertising, you can effectively promote your affiliate products or services to a highly targeted audience, increasing the likelihood of conversions and boosting your income.

Mobile-friendly email marketing is another essential component of mobile optimization for affiliate marketers. With the majority of people checking their emails on their mobile devices, it is crucial to ensure that your email campaigns are optimized for mobile viewing. This includes using responsive email templates, optimizing subject lines and preheaders for mobile screens, and ensuring that your call-to-action buttons are easily clickable on smaller screens. By delivering mobile-friendly emails, you can enhance engagement and increase the chances of conversions.

In conclusion, mobile optimization is of utmost importance for affiliate marketers looking to earn a six-figure income. With the increasing dominance of mobile devices in internet usage, failing to optimize your website and marketing materials for mobile can result in missed opportunities and lower earnings. By prioritizing mobile optimization, you can improve your search engine rankings, enhance user engagement, tap into the growing m-commerce market, and effectively reach your target audience through mobile advertising and email marketing. Embracing mobile optimization is a crucial step towards achieving success in the competitive world of affiliate marketing.

8.2 Responsive Web Design

In today's digital age, mobile devices have become an integral part of our lives. People are increasingly using their smartphones and tablets to browse the internet, shop online, and interact with content. As an affiliate marketer, it is crucial to optimize your website for mobile devices to ensure a seamless user experience and maximize your earning potential. This is where responsive web design comes into play.

Responsive web design is an approach to web development that aims to create websites that adapt and respond to different screen sizes and devices. It ensures that your website looks and functions well on desktop computers, laptops, tablets, and smartphones. By implementing responsive web design, you can provide a consistent and user-friendly experience to your visitors, regardless of the device they are using.

1. **Mobile Usage is on the Rise**: The number of people accessing the internet through mobile devices is increasing rapidly. According to Statista, mobile devices accounted for over 50% of global website traffic in 2020. By optimizing your website for mobile devices, you can tap into this growing market and reach a larger audience.

2. **Improved User Experience**: Responsive web design ensures that your website is easy to navigate, read, and interact with on any device. It eliminates the need for users to zoom in or scroll horizontally, providing a seamless and enjoyable browsing experience. A positive user experience leads to increased engagement, longer visit durations, and higher conversion rates.

3. **Better Search Engine Rankings**: Search engines like Google prioritize mobile-friendly websites in their search results. Having a responsive website can improve your search engine optimization (SEO) efforts and help you rank higher in mobile search results. This, in turn, can drive more organic traffic to your website and increase your chances of earning affiliate commissions.

4. **Consistent Branding**: With responsive web design, your website's branding elements, such as logos, colors, and fonts, remain consistent across different devices. This helps in building a strong and recognizable brand identity, which is crucial for establishing trust and credibility with your audience.

To create a responsive website, you need to follow certain principles and best practices. Here are some key principles of responsive web design:

1. **Fluid Grids**: Instead of using fixed pixel-based layouts, responsive web design utilizes fluid grids that automatically adjust to the screen size. This ensures that the website's layout and content adapt seamlessly to different devices.

2. **Flexible Images and Media**: Images and media elements should also be flexible and adapt to different screen sizes. This can be achieved by using CSS techniques such as max-width: 100% to ensure that images scale proportionally.

3. **Media Queries**: Media queries allow you to apply different styles and layouts based on the characteristics of the device, such as screen size, resolution, and orientation. By using media queries, you can create a customized user experience for each device.

4. **Mobile-First Approach**: Adopting a mobile-first approach means designing and developing your website with mobile devices in mind from the start. This ensures that your website is optimized for mobile devices and then progressively enhanced for larger screens.

5. **Touch-Friendly Navigation**: Mobile devices rely on touch-based interactions, so it is essential to design navigation menus and buttons that are easy to tap and navigate. Avoid using small buttons or links that are difficult to click on smaller screens.

Implementing Responsive Web Design

To implement responsive web design, you have a few options:

1. **Use a Responsive Website Template**: Many website builders and content management systems (CMS) offer responsive templates that you can use as a starting point. These templates are already optimized for different screen sizes and devices, allowing you to create a responsive website without extensive coding knowledge.

2. **Customize an Existing Website**: If you already have a website, you can hire a web developer or use responsive frameworks like Bootstrap or Foundation to make your website responsive. This involves modifying the existing codebase to incorporate responsive design principles.

3. **Hire a Web Designer/Developer**: If you prefer a more customized approach, you can hire a professional web designer or developer to create a responsive website from scratch. They will ensure that your website is tailored to your specific needs and optimized for all devices.

Testing and Optimization

Once you have implemented responsive web design, it is crucial to test your website on different devices and screen sizes to ensure that it functions as intended. This involves using emulators, physical devices, or browser developer tools to simulate various devices and screen resolutions.

Regular testing and optimization are essential to identify any issues or areas for improvement. Pay attention to factors such as page load speed, readability, and ease of navigation. By continuously monitoring and optimizing your website's performance, you can provide the best possible user experience and maximize your affiliate marketing success.

In conclusion, responsive web design is a critical aspect of affiliate marketing in today's mobile-driven world. By optimizing your website for mobile devices, you can reach a wider audience, improve user experience, and increase your chances of earning a six-figure income. Implementing responsive web design principles and testing your website on different devices will ensure that your website remains user-friendly and effective across all platforms.

8.3 Mobile Advertising Strategies

In today's digital age, mobile devices have become an integral part of our lives. People are constantly glued to their smartphones, tablets, and other mobile devices, making it a prime platform for advertising. As an affiliate marketer, it is crucial to tap into the potential of mobile advertising to maximize your reach and increase your affiliate sales. In this section, we will explore effective mobile advertising strategies that can help you earn a six-figure income per month.

Understanding the Power of Mobile Advertising

Mobile advertising refers to the practice of promoting products or services through mobile devices such as smartphones and tablets. With the increasing number of mobile users worldwide, mobile advertising has become a powerful tool for affiliate marketers to connect with their target audience. Here are some reasons why mobile advertising is essential for your affiliate marketing success:

1. **Wider Reach**: Mobile devices have a broader reach compared to traditional desktop computers. People carry their smartphones with them everywhere, allowing you to reach them anytime and anywhere.

2. **Higher Engagement**: Mobile users tend to be more engaged with their devices, spending a significant amount of time browsing the internet, using apps, and interacting on social media. This high level of engagement presents an opportunity for you to capture their attention and promote your affiliate offers effectively.

3. **Targeted Advertising**: Mobile advertising platforms provide advanced targeting options, allowing you to reach specific demographics, locations, and interests. This targeted approach ensures that your ads are shown to the right audience, increasing the chances of conversions.

4. **Cost-Effective**: Mobile advertising can be cost-effective, especially when compared to traditional advertising methods. With a relatively small investment, you can reach a large number of potential customers and generate substantial affiliate income.

Choosing the Right Mobile Advertising Channels

To effectively leverage mobile advertising, it is crucial to choose the right channels that align with your target audience and niche. Here are some popular mobile advertising channels that you can consider:

1. **Mobile Apps**: Advertising within mobile apps is an effective way to reach a highly engaged audience. You can explore popular app advertising platforms such as Google AdMob, Facebook Audience Network, and Apple Search Ads to promote your affiliate offers.

2. **Mobile Websites**: Mobile websites provide an opportunity to display banner ads, interstitial ads, or native ads to mobile users. You can partner with mobile ad networks like Google AdSense, Media.net, or PropellerAds to monetize your mobile website traffic.

3. **Social Media Advertising**: Social media platforms such as Facebook, Instagram, Twitter, and LinkedIn offer robust mobile advertising options. These platforms allow you to target specific demographics, interests, and behaviors, ensuring that your ads are shown to the right audience.

4. **Mobile Search Advertising**: Mobile search advertising involves displaying ads on search engine results pages (SERPs) when users search for specific keywords. Platforms like Google Ads and Bing Ads provide mobile-specific ad formats and targeting options to help you reach mobile users effectively.

Crafting Effective Mobile Ads

Once you have chosen the right mobile advertising channels, it is essential to create compelling and engaging ads that resonate with your target audience. Here are some tips for crafting effective mobile ads:

1. **Keep it Concise**: Mobile screens have limited space, so it is crucial to keep your ad copy concise and to the point. Use clear and compelling language to grab the user's attention and convey your message effectively.

2. **Use Eye-Catching Visuals**: Visuals play a significant role in mobile advertising. Use high-quality images or videos that are visually appealing and relevant to your affiliate offer. Ensure that your visuals are optimized for mobile devices to provide the best user experience.

3. **Include a Strong Call-to-Action (CTA)**: A strong CTA is essential to encourage users to take action. Use action-oriented words and phrases that create a sense of urgency and clearly communicate what you want the user to do.

4. **Optimize for Mobile Devices**: Ensure that your ads are optimized for mobile devices by using responsive design and mobile-friendly formats. Test your ads on different mobile devices to ensure they are displayed correctly and provide a seamless user experience.

Tracking and Analyzing Mobile Advertising Performance

To measure the effectiveness of your mobile advertising campaigns, it is crucial to track and analyze key performance indicators (KPIs). Here are some important metrics to consider:

1. **Click-Through Rate (CTR)**: CTR measures the percentage of users who click on your ad after seeing it. A higher CTR indicates that your ad is engaging and resonating with your target audience.

2. **Conversion Rate**: Conversion rate measures the percentage of users who complete a desired action, such as making a purchase or signing up for a newsletter. Tracking conversions will help you determine the effectiveness of your mobile ads in generating affiliate sales.

3. **Return on Ad Spend (ROAS)**: ROAS measures the revenue generated for every dollar spent on advertising. It helps you evaluate the profitability of your mobile advertising campaigns and make informed decisions about budget allocation.

4. **Engagement Metrics**: Engagement metrics such as time spent on site, page views, and bounce rate can provide insights into how users interact with your mobile ads and website. Analyzing these metrics will help you optimize your campaigns for better results.

Optimizing Mobile Advertising Campaigns

To maximize your affiliate income through mobile advertising, it is essential to continuously optimize your campaigns. Here are some optimization strategies to consider:

1. **A/B Testing**: Conduct A/B tests by creating multiple versions of your ads and landing pages to identify the most effective elements. Test different ad copy, visuals, CTAs, and landing page designs to improve your conversion rates.

2. **Retargeting**: Implement retargeting campaigns to reach users who have previously shown interest in your affiliate offers. By displaying personalized ads to these users, you can increase the chances of conversions and maximize your ROI.

3. **Ad Placement Optimization**: Monitor the performance of your ads on different mobile advertising channels and optimize their placement. Focus on channels and placements that generate the highest engagement and conversions.

4. **Continuous Monitoring and Analysis**: Regularly monitor the performance of your mobile advertising campaigns and analyze the data to identify areas for improvement. Make data-driven decisions to optimize your campaigns and achieve better results.

By implementing effective mobile advertising strategies, you can tap into the vast potential of mobile devices and significantly increase your affiliate income. Remember to choose the right mobile advertising channels, craft compelling ads, track performance metrics, and continuously optimize your campaigns for maximum success. With dedication, perseverance, and the right strategies, earning a six-figure income per month through affiliate marketing is within your reach.

8.4 Mobile-Friendly Email Marketing

In today's digital age, mobile devices have become an integral part of our lives. People are constantly connected to their smartphones and tablets, making it crucial for affiliate marketers to optimize their strategies for mobile devices. One of the most effective ways to reach and engage with your audience on mobile is through email marketing. In this section, we will explore the importance of mobile-friendly email marketing and provide you with actionable tips to maximize your affiliate sales.

The Rise of Mobile Email Usage

With the increasing popularity of smartphones, the way people consume email has drastically changed. According to recent statistics, more than 50% of emails are now opened on mobile devices. This shift in consumer behavior highlights the importance of optimizing your email marketing campaigns for mobile users.

Responsive Email Design

To ensure your emails are mobile-friendly, it is essential to use responsive email design. Responsive design allows your emails to adapt and display correctly on different screen sizes and devices. By using responsive templates or designing your emails with mobile users in mind, you can provide a seamless experience for your subscribers.

Here are some key elements to consider when creating mobile-friendly emails:

1. **Simplified Layout**: Mobile screens are smaller, so it's important to keep your email layout clean and simple. Avoid cluttered designs and focus on delivering a clear and concise message.

2. **Large Fonts and Buttons**: Make sure your text is easily readable on mobile devices by using larger fonts. Similarly, use larger buttons that are easy to tap with a finger. This will improve the overall user experience and increase the chances of engagement.

3. **Single Column Format**: Opt for a single column layout in your emails to ensure they are easily scrollable on mobile devices. This format eliminates the need for horizontal scrolling, making it more convenient for your subscribers.

4. **Optimize Images**: Images can significantly impact the loading time of your emails on mobile devices. Compress and optimize your images to reduce file size without compromising quality. This will help your emails load quickly and improve the user experience.

5. **Clear Call-to-Action**: Your call-to-action (CTA) buttons should be prominently displayed and easily clickable on mobile devices. Use contrasting colors and compelling copy to encourage your subscribers to take action.

In addition to the design, the content of your emails should also be optimized for mobile users. Here are some tips to ensure your email content is mobile-friendly:

1. **Keep it Concise**: Mobile users have limited attention spans, so keep your email content concise and to the point. Use short paragraphs, bullet points, and subheadings to make your emails scannable and easy to read.

2. **Personalization**: Personalize your emails by addressing your subscribers by their first name. This simple touch can make your emails feel more personalized and increase engagement.

3. **Mobile-Friendly Links**: Ensure that any links you include in your emails are mobile-friendly. Test the links on different devices to ensure they are easily clickable and lead to mobile-optimized landing pages.

4. **Avoid Excessive Images**: While images can enhance the visual appeal of your emails, too many images can slow down loading times and distract from your message. Use images strategically and make sure they are relevant to the content.

5. **Preview and Test**: Before sending out your emails, preview them on different mobile devices and email clients to ensure they display correctly. Testing is crucial to identify any formatting issues or broken elements that may affect the user experience.

To streamline your mobile email marketing efforts, consider implementing automation. Automation allows you to send targeted and personalized emails to your subscribers based on their behavior and preferences. By leveraging automation tools, you can create a series of mobile-friendly emails that nurture and engage your audience throughout their customer journey.

Here are some examples of mobile email automation:

1. **Welcome Emails**: Send a personalized welcome email to new subscribers, introducing them to your brand and providing valuable content or offers.

2. **Abandoned Cart Emails**: If a subscriber adds items to their cart but doesn't complete the purchase, send them a reminder email with a mobile-friendly link to their cart.

3. **Re-Engagement Emails**: If a subscriber hasn't engaged with your emails for a while, send them a re-engagement email with a compelling offer or content to encourage them to interact with your brand again.

4. **Upsell and Cross-Sell Emails**: Based on a subscriber's previous purchases or browsing behavior, send them targeted emails promoting related products or services.

To optimize your mobile email marketing strategy, it's crucial to track and analyze the performance of your campaigns. By monitoring key metrics, you can identify areas for improvement and make data-driven decisions.

Here are some important metrics to track:

1. **Open Rate**: Measure the percentage of subscribers who open your emails on mobile devices. This metric indicates the effectiveness of your subject lines and email preview text.

2. **Click-Through Rate (CTR)**: Track the percentage of subscribers who click on links within your emails. A high CTR indicates that your content and CTAs are engaging and compelling.

3. **Conversion Rate**: Measure the percentage of subscribers who complete a desired action, such as making a purchase or signing up for a newsletter. This metric helps you evaluate the effectiveness of your email content and calls-to-action.

4. **Bounce Rate**: Monitor the percentage of emails that are undeliverable or bounce back. A high bounce rate may indicate issues with your email list quality or deliverability.

By regularly analyzing these metrics, you can identify trends, optimize your email campaigns, and improve your overall mobile email marketing performance.

In conclusion, mobile-friendly email marketing is a powerful tool for affiliate marketers to engage with their audience and drive affiliate sales. By implementing responsive design, optimizing your email content, and leveraging automation, you can create compelling mobile experiences that resonate with your subscribers. Remember to track and analyze your email performance to continuously improve your mobile email marketing strategy.

Scaling Your Affiliate Marketing Business

9.1 Automating Your Affiliate Marketing Processes

As your affiliate marketing business grows, it becomes essential to find ways to streamline and automate your processes. Automation not only saves you time and effort but also allows you to scale your business and increase your earning potential. In this section, we will explore various strategies and tools that can help you automate your affiliate marketing processes and maximize your income.

Automation offers several benefits for affiliate marketers, including:

1. **Time-saving**: By automating repetitive tasks, you can free up your time to focus on more important aspects of your business, such as creating content, building relationships, and expanding into new niches.

2. **Scalability**: Automation allows you to scale your business without being limited by your time and resources. With the right systems in place, you can handle a larger volume of traffic, leads, and sales.

3. **Consistency**: Automation ensures that your processes are executed consistently, reducing the risk of errors and providing a seamless experience for your audience.

4. **Efficiency**: By automating tasks, you can accomplish them faster and more efficiently, increasing your productivity and allowing you to accomplish more in less time.

Automating Your Affiliate Marketing Processes

Here are some key areas of your affiliate marketing business that you can automate:

1. Email Marketing

Email marketing is a crucial component of affiliate marketing, and automating your email campaigns can significantly enhance your results. Consider the following automation strategies:

- **Autoresponders**: Set up a series of automated emails that are triggered when someone subscribes to your email list. These emails can provide valuable content, build trust, and promote your affiliate products.

- **Segmentation**: Use email marketing software to segment your subscribers based on their interests, behavior, or demographics. This allows you to send targeted emails that are more likely to resonate with your audience and drive conversions.

- **Drip Campaigns**: Create automated drip campaigns that deliver a sequence of emails over a specific period. These campaigns can be used to nurture leads, promote products, or provide educational content.

2. Social Media Management

Social media platforms are powerful tools for promoting your affiliate products and engaging with your audience. Automating your social media management can save you time and ensure consistent posting. Consider the following automation strategies:

- **Scheduling Tools**: Use social media scheduling tools like Hootsuite or Buffer to schedule your posts in advance. This allows you to maintain a consistent presence on social media without having to manually post every day.

- **Content Curation**: Use tools like Feedly or Pocket to curate relevant content from various sources. You can then automate the sharing of this content on your social media profiles, providing value to your audience and establishing yourself as an authority in your niche.

- **Social Media Automation Tools**: Consider using automation tools like IFTTT or Zapier to automate repetitive tasks on social media, such as following new followers, sending direct messages, or reposting content.

3. Content Creation and Publishing

Creating and publishing content is a time-consuming task, but automation can help streamline the process. Consider the following automation strategies:

- **Content Curation**: Use tools like BuzzSumo or Google Alerts to discover trending topics and popular content in your niche. This can help you generate ideas for your own content and stay up-to-date with industry trends.

- **Content Management Systems**: Utilize content management systems like WordPress or Joomla to automate the publishing of your blog posts or articles. These platforms allow you to schedule posts in advance, ensuring a consistent flow of content.

- **Content Repurposing**: Repurpose your existing content into different formats, such as videos, podcasts, or infographics. This allows you to reach a wider audience and maximize the value of your content.

4. Affiliate Link Management

Managing your affiliate links can be a tedious task, especially if you promote multiple products or work with different affiliate networks. Consider the following automation strategies:

- **Link Shorteners**: Use link shortening tools like Bitly or Pretty Links to create shortened, trackable links for your affiliate promotions. These tools provide analytics and allow you to easily manage and update your links.

- **Link Cloaking**: Consider using link cloaking plugins or software to mask your affiliate links. This not only makes your links more visually appealing but also protects your affiliate commissions from theft or hijacking.

- **Link Rotators**: If you promote multiple products or work with different affiliate networks, consider using link rotators to automatically rotate and distribute your affiliate links. This allows you to test different offers and maximize your earnings.

Conclusion

Automating your affiliate marketing processes is essential for scaling your business and maximizing your income. By leveraging automation tools and strategies, you can save time, increase efficiency, and ensure consistency in your marketing efforts. Whether it's automating your email campaigns, social media management, content creation, or affiliate link management, there are numerous opportunities to streamline your processes and achieve six-figure income potential in affiliate marketing.

9.2 Outsourcing Tasks and Hiring Virtual Assistants

As your affiliate marketing business grows, you may find yourself overwhelmed with the increasing workload. To continue scaling your business and maintain your focus on high-value tasks, it's essential to outsource certain tasks and consider hiring virtual assistants. Outsourcing can help you save time, increase productivity, and ultimately contribute to your goal of earning a six-figure income per month. In this section, we will explore the benefits of outsourcing, how to identify tasks to outsource, and the process of hiring virtual assistants.

The Benefits of Outsourcing

Outsourcing tasks and hiring virtual assistants can provide numerous benefits for your affiliate marketing business. Here are some key advantages:

1. **Time-saving**: By delegating repetitive or time-consuming tasks to others, you can free up your time to focus on strategic activities that directly contribute to your income generation.

2. **Increased productivity**: Outsourcing allows you to leverage the expertise of others, enabling you to complete tasks more efficiently and effectively.

3. **Scalability**: As your business grows, outsourcing becomes crucial for scaling your operations. By delegating tasks, you can handle a higher volume of work without sacrificing quality.

4. **Access to specialized skills**: Hiring virtual assistants with specific skills can bring expertise to areas where you may lack proficiency, such as graphic design, content writing, or social media management.

5. **Cost-effectiveness**: Outsourcing can be a cost-effective solution compared to hiring full-time employees. Virtual assistants often work on a project or hourly basis, allowing you to control your expenses.

Identifying Tasks to Outsource

To determine which tasks to outsource, start by evaluating your strengths and weaknesses. Identify the tasks that you find time-consuming or those that you struggle with. These are the areas where outsourcing can have the most significant impact. Here are some common tasks that affiliate marketers often outsource:

1. **Content creation**: Writing blog posts, creating social media content, and producing videos can be time-consuming. Outsourcing these tasks to skilled writers or content creators can help you consistently produce high-quality content.

2. **Graphic design**: If you lack design skills, outsourcing graphic design tasks such as creating banners, logos, or infographics can enhance the visual appeal of your website and marketing materials.

3. **Website development and maintenance**: If you're not proficient in web development, hiring a virtual assistant or freelancer to handle website setup, maintenance, and troubleshooting can save you time and ensure your site runs smoothly.

4. **Search engine optimization (SEO)**: SEO is crucial for driving organic traffic to your website. Outsourcing SEO tasks, such as keyword research, on-page optimization, and link building, can help improve your website's visibility in search engine results.

5. **Social media management**: Managing multiple social media accounts can be time-consuming. Outsourcing social media tasks, including content creation, scheduling posts, and engaging with followers, can help you maintain an active online presence.

6. **Customer support**: As your business grows, handling customer inquiries and support can become overwhelming. Outsourcing customer support tasks to virtual assistants can ensure timely and efficient responses to customer queries.

Hiring Virtual Assistants

When hiring virtual assistants, it's essential to follow a systematic process to find the right candidates for your business. Here are some steps to consider:

1. **Define your requirements**: Clearly outline the tasks and skills you need assistance with. This will help you create a job description and attract suitable candidates.

2. **Post job listings**: Utilize online platforms such as freelancing websites, job boards, or social media groups to advertise your job openings. Be specific about the skills and experience you're looking for.

3. **Review applications**: Carefully review the applications and resumes you receive. Look for candidates with relevant experience, positive reviews or testimonials, and good communication skills.

4. **Conduct interviews**: Shortlist the most promising candidates and conduct interviews to assess their suitability for the role. Ask questions about their experience, availability, and ability to handle the tasks you require.

5. **Check references**: Contact the references provided by the candidates to verify their skills, work ethic, and reliability.

6. **Trial period**: Consider starting with a trial period to evaluate the virtual assistant's performance and compatibility with your business. This allows you to assess their abilities before committing to a long-term arrangement.

7. **Establish clear communication**: Once you've hired a virtual assistant, establish clear communication channels and expectations. Regularly communicate your goals, provide feedback, and ensure they have the necessary resources to complete their tasks.

Remember, outsourcing tasks and hiring virtual assistants is an ongoing process. As your business evolves, you may need to adjust your outsourcing strategy and hire additional help to meet your growing needs.

By effectively outsourcing tasks and hiring virtual assistants, you can focus on high-value activities that directly contribute to your affiliate marketing success. This strategic approach will help you scale your business, increase productivity, and ultimately work towards earning a six-figure income per month.

9.3 Expanding into New Niches and Markets

Expanding into new niches and markets is a crucial step in scaling your affiliate marketing business and increasing your income potential. By diversifying your portfolio and targeting different audiences, you can tap into new sources of revenue and maximize your earning potential. In this section, we will explore the strategies and considerations involved in expanding into new niches and markets.

Understanding the Importance of Market Research

Before venturing into new niches and markets, it is essential to conduct thorough market research. This research will help you identify profitable opportunities and understand the needs and preferences of your target audience. By gaining insights into the market landscape, you can make informed decisions and develop effective marketing strategies.

Start by identifying potential niches that align with your interests, expertise, and existing affiliate marketing efforts. Look for niches that have a high demand for products or services and a relatively low level of competition. This combination will increase your chances of success and allow you to stand out in the market.

Evaluating Market Potential

Once you have identified potential niches, it is crucial to evaluate their market potential. Look for indicators such as market size, growth rate, and consumer spending patterns. Conduct competitor analysis to understand the existing players in the market and their strategies.

Consider the profitability of the niche by researching the average commission rates and the potential for high-ticket sales. Look for niches that offer a good balance between demand and competition, allowing you to earn substantial commissions while still having room to grow.

Conducting Keyword Research

Keyword research is an essential part of expanding into new niches and markets. By identifying the keywords that your target audience is using to search for products or services, you can optimize your content and increase your visibility in search engine results.

Use keyword research tools to identify relevant keywords with a high search volume and low competition. These keywords will help you create content that resonates with your target audience and attracts organic traffic to your website. Incorporate these keywords strategically into your website content, blog posts, and product reviews to improve your search engine rankings.

Creating New Content and Promotional Strategies

Expanding into new niches and markets requires creating new content and promotional strategies tailored to the specific audience. Conduct thorough research to understand the pain points, desires, and preferences of your target audience in the new niche.

Create high-quality content that addresses the needs and interests of your target audience. This could include informative blog posts, engaging videos, or in-depth product reviews. Tailor your content to the new niche, showcasing your expertise and providing value to your audience.

Develop promotional strategies that resonate with the new audience. This could include leveraging social media platforms, collaborating with influencers in the niche, or running targeted advertising campaigns. Experiment with different strategies and track their performance to identify the most effective approaches.

Building Relationships with New Affiliate Programs

Expanding into new niches and markets often involves partnering with new affiliate programs. Research and identify reputable affiliate programs that offer products or services relevant to your new niche. Look for programs that provide competitive commission rates, reliable tracking systems, and excellent support for affiliates.

When joining new affiliate programs, carefully review their terms and conditions to ensure they align with your business goals and strategies. Pay attention to commission structures, payment schedules, and any restrictions or limitations that may impact your promotional efforts.

Testing and Optimization

As you expand into new niches and markets, it is essential to continuously test and optimize your strategies. Monitor the performance of your content, promotional campaigns, and affiliate programs to identify areas for improvement.

Track key performance indicators (KPIs) such as click-through rates, conversion rates, and revenue generated. Analyze the data to identify trends, patterns, and areas of underperformance. Use this information to make data-driven decisions and optimize your strategies for better results.

Consider conducting split tests to compare different approaches and determine the most effective strategies. Test different headlines, calls-to-action, landing page designs, and promotional channels to identify the best combination for maximizing conversions and revenue.

Conclusion

Expanding into new niches and markets is a powerful strategy for scaling your affiliate marketing business and increasing your income potential. By conducting thorough market research, evaluating market potential, and creating targeted content and promotional strategies, you can tap into new sources of revenue and reach a wider audience.

Building relationships with new affiliate programs and continuously testing and optimizing your strategies will help you stay ahead of the competition and maximize your earning potential. Remember to track your performance, analyze the data, and make data-driven decisions to ensure long-term success in your affiliate marketing endeavors.

9.4 Building Relationships with Affiliate Networks

Affiliate marketing is a powerful business model that allows individuals to earn a significant income by promoting products or services and earning a commission for each sale made through their affiliate links. To truly unleash the potential of affiliate marketing and achieve a six-figure income per month, it is crucial to build strong relationships with affiliate networks. These networks act as intermediaries between affiliates and merchants, providing a platform for affiliates to find and promote products and for merchants to reach a wider audience. In this section, we will explore the importance of building relationships with affiliate networks and provide strategies to establish and nurture these connections.

Building relationships with affiliate networks can bring numerous benefits to your affiliate marketing business. Here are some key advantages:

1. **Access to High-Quality Affiliate Programs:** Affiliate networks have a wide range of affiliate programs available, including those from reputable and well-established merchants. By building relationships with these networks, you gain access to a diverse selection of high-quality affiliate programs that can help you maximize your earnings potential.

2. **Exclusive Offers and Promotions:** Affiliate networks often provide exclusive offers and promotions to their trusted affiliates. By establishing strong relationships with these networks, you may gain access to special deals, higher commission rates, or unique promotional opportunities that can give you a competitive edge in the market.

3. **Timely Communication and Support:** Affiliate networks act as a bridge between affiliates and merchants, facilitating communication and providing support when needed. By building relationships with these networks, you can expect timely updates on new products, changes in commission rates, and any other important information that can impact your affiliate marketing efforts.

4. **Trust and Credibility:** Building relationships with affiliate networks helps establish trust and credibility in the industry. When you have a strong connection with a reputable network, it reflects positively on your own brand and reputation as an affiliate marketer. This can lead to increased trust from your audience and potential customers, ultimately driving more conversions and higher earnings.

Strategies for Building Relationships with Affiliate Networks

Now that we understand the benefits of building relationships with affiliate networks, let's explore some effective strategies to establish and nurture these connections:

1. Research and Choose the Right Affiliate Networks

Not all affiliate networks are created equal. It is essential to research and choose the right networks that align with your niche and business goals. Look for networks that have a solid reputation, a wide range of affiliate programs, and excellent support for their affiliates. Consider factors such as commission rates, payment terms, tracking technology, and the overall user experience of the network's platform.

2. Provide Value and Build Trust

Affiliate networks value affiliates who provide value to their merchants. Focus on building trust and credibility by consistently delivering high-quality content, promoting products that align with your audience's needs, and providing honest and unbiased reviews. By demonstrating your expertise and commitment to your audience, you will gain the trust of both the network and the merchants they represent.

3. Engage with Affiliate Managers

Affiliate managers play a crucial role in affiliate networks. They are responsible for managing relationships with affiliates and merchants, providing support, and ensuring the smooth operation of the network. Take the initiative to engage with affiliate managers by introducing yourself, asking questions, and seeking guidance. Building a personal connection with affiliate managers can lead to valuable insights, exclusive opportunities, and a stronger relationship with the network.

4. Attend Affiliate Marketing Events and Conferences

Affiliate marketing events and conferences provide excellent opportunities to network with industry professionals, including representatives from affiliate networks. These events often feature panel discussions, workshops, and networking sessions where you can connect with affiliate managers and learn about the latest trends and strategies in the industry. By attending these events, you can establish face-to-face connections and build relationships that go beyond online interactions.

5. Provide Feedback and Suggestions

Affiliate networks appreciate feedback from their affiliates. If you encounter any issues or have suggestions for improvement, don't hesitate to communicate with the network's support team or affiliate managers. By providing constructive feedback, you demonstrate your commitment to the success of the network and contribute to its continuous improvement. This proactive approach can help strengthen your relationship with the network and position you as a valuable affiliate partner.

6. Stay Updated with Network News and Updates

Affiliate networks often share important news, updates, and promotional opportunities through their newsletters, blogs, or social media channels. Make sure to stay updated with the latest information from the networks you are affiliated with. By being aware of new product launches, changes in commission rates, or upcoming promotions, you can optimize your marketing strategies and take advantage of timely opportunities to boost your earnings.

7. Be Professional and Reliable

Professionalism and reliability are key attributes that affiliate networks value in their affiliates. Always meet deadlines, adhere to the network's terms and conditions, and maintain open and honest communication. By being a reliable affiliate, you build trust and credibility with the network, increasing your chances of accessing exclusive offers and receiving support when needed.

Building relationships with affiliate networks is not a one-time effort. It requires ongoing nurturing and maintenance. Continuously engage with the network, provide feedback, and stay updated with their news and updates. By fostering long-term relationships, you position yourself as a trusted and valuable affiliate partner, increasing your chances of accessing new opportunities and maximizing your affiliate marketing income.

In conclusion, building relationships with affiliate networks is a crucial aspect of achieving success in affiliate marketing. By accessing high-quality affiliate programs, gaining exclusive offers, receiving timely support, and establishing trust and credibility, you can unlock the full potential of your affiliate marketing business. Implement the strategies outlined in this section to build strong and lasting connections with affiliate networks, and watch your income soar to six-figure levels.

Tracking and Analyzing Affiliate Marketing Performance

10.1 Setting Up Tracking Systems

In order to effectively track and analyze the performance of your affiliate marketing campaigns, it is crucial to set up tracking systems. These systems will provide you with valuable data and insights that will help you optimize your strategies and maximize your earnings. In this section, we will explore the importance of tracking systems and discuss how to set them up for your affiliate marketing business.

Why Tracking Systems are Important

Tracking systems play a vital role in affiliate marketing as they allow you to monitor the performance of your campaigns and make data-driven decisions. Here are some key reasons why setting up tracking systems is crucial for your success:

1. **Performance Evaluation**: Tracking systems enable you to measure the effectiveness of your marketing efforts. By monitoring key metrics such as click-through rates, conversion rates, and revenue generated, you can identify which campaigns are performing well and which ones need improvement.

2. **Identifying Profitable Channels**: With tracking systems in place, you can determine which traffic sources and marketing channels are driving the most conversions and revenue. This information will help you allocate your resources effectively and focus on the channels that yield the highest returns.

3. **Optimization Opportunities**: Tracking systems provide valuable insights into user behavior and preferences. By analyzing data such as bounce rates, time on site, and page views, you can identify areas for improvement and optimize your website and marketing strategies accordingly.

4. **ROI Calculation**: Tracking systems allow you to calculate the return on investment (ROI) for your affiliate marketing campaigns. By comparing the revenue generated with the costs incurred, you can determine the profitability of your campaigns and make informed decisions about resource allocation.

Setting Up Tracking Systems

Now that you understand the importance of tracking systems, let's discuss how to set them up for your affiliate marketing business. Here are the key steps involved:

1. **Choose a Tracking Platform**: There are several tracking platforms available in the market, each offering different features and capabilities. Research and choose a platform that suits your needs and budget. Some popular options include Google Analytics, ClickMagick, and Voluum.

2. **Set Up Conversion Tracking**: Conversion tracking is essential for measuring the success of your affiliate marketing campaigns. It allows you to track the actions taken by users, such as making a purchase or filling out a form. Most tracking platforms provide instructions on how to set up conversion tracking, which usually involves adding a tracking code to your website.

3. **Create Unique Tracking Links**: To track the performance of individual campaigns, it is important to create unique tracking links for each affiliate offer or promotion. These links will contain a tracking code that identifies the traffic source and campaign. Most tracking platforms offer tools to generate these links automatically.

4. **Implement Sub-IDs**: Sub-IDs are additional tracking parameters that can be added to your tracking links. They allow you to further segment and analyze your traffic. For example, you can use sub-IDs to track the performance of different ad placements or keywords. Consult your tracking platform's documentation for instructions on how to implement sub-IDs.

5. **Test and Verify Tracking**: After setting up your tracking systems, it is crucial to test and verify that they are working correctly. Click on your tracking links and ensure that the data is being recorded accurately in your tracking platform. This step is essential to ensure the reliability of your data and avoid any tracking issues.

6. **Analyze and Optimize**: Once your tracking systems are up and running, regularly analyze the data to gain insights into the performance of your campaigns. Look for patterns, trends, and areas for improvement. Use this information to optimize your strategies, refine your targeting, and maximize your conversions and revenue.

By setting up tracking systems and diligently analyzing the data they provide, you will be able to make informed decisions and optimize your affiliate marketing campaigns for maximum profitability. Remember, tracking is an ongoing process, and it is important to regularly monitor and adjust your strategies based on the insights gained from your tracking systems.

10.2 Analyzing Key Performance Indicators (KPIs)

Once you have set up your tracking systems to monitor the performance of your affiliate marketing campaigns, it is crucial to analyze the key performance indicators (KPIs) to understand how well your strategies are working. By regularly reviewing and interpreting these metrics, you can make informed decisions to optimize your campaigns and maximize your affiliate sales. In this section, we will explore the essential KPIs that you should focus on and how to analyze them effectively.

Understanding Key Performance Indicators (KPIs)

Key performance indicators are measurable values that indicate the success or effectiveness of a particular activity or campaign. In the context of affiliate marketing, KPIs help you evaluate the performance of your promotional efforts, track your progress towards your income goals, and identify areas for improvement. By monitoring these metrics, you can gain valuable insights into the effectiveness of your strategies and make data-driven decisions to optimize your campaigns.

Essential KPIs for Affiliate Marketing

1. **Conversion Rate**: The conversion rate is one of the most critical KPIs in affiliate marketing. It measures the percentage of visitors who take the desired action, such as making a purchase or signing up for a newsletter. A high conversion rate indicates that your marketing efforts are effective in persuading visitors to become customers. To calculate the conversion rate, divide the number of conversions by the total number of visitors and multiply by 100.

2. **Click-Through Rate (CTR)**: The click-through rate measures the percentage of people who click on your affiliate links or ads compared to the total number of impressions. A high CTR indicates that your promotional content is compelling and engaging, attracting the attention of your target audience. To calculate the CTR, divide the number of clicks by the number of impressions and multiply by 100.

3. **Average Order Value (AOV)**: The average order value represents the average amount of money spent by customers in a single transaction. A higher AOV indicates that your audience is purchasing higher-priced products or multiple items, which can significantly impact your overall earnings. To calculate the AOV, divide the total revenue by the number of orders.

4. **Return on Investment (ROI)**: ROI measures the profitability of your affiliate marketing campaigns by comparing the amount of money you have earned to the amount you have invested. A positive ROI indicates that your campaigns are generating more revenue than the costs incurred. To calculate the ROI, subtract

the total costs from the total revenue, divide the result by the total costs, and multiply by 100.

5. **Earnings per Click (EPC)**: EPC measures the average amount of money you earn for each click on your affiliate links. It helps you evaluate the profitability of your campaigns and compare the performance of different affiliate programs or products. To calculate the EPC, divide the total earnings by the total number of clicks.

6. **Bounce Rate**: The bounce rate represents the percentage of visitors who leave your website after viewing only one page. A high bounce rate may indicate that your website or landing page is not engaging enough or fails to meet visitors' expectations. By reducing the bounce rate, you can increase the chances of converting visitors into customers. To calculate the bounce rate, divide the number of single-page visits by the total number of visits and multiply by 100.

7. **Customer Lifetime Value (CLTV)**: CLTV measures the total revenue generated by a customer throughout their entire relationship with your business. By understanding the CLTV, you can determine the long-term value of acquiring and retaining customers. This metric is particularly important in affiliate marketing, as it helps you assess the profitability of your promotional efforts. To calculate the CLTV, multiply the average purchase value by the average purchase frequency and the average customer lifespan.

Analyzing KPIs and Making Data-Driven Decisions

To effectively analyze your KPIs and make data-driven decisions, follow these steps:

1. **Set benchmarks**: Establish benchmarks for each KPI based on industry standards or your own performance goals. These benchmarks will serve as a reference point to evaluate your performance and identify areas for improvement.

2. **Regularly monitor and track**: Continuously monitor and track your KPIs using the tracking systems you have set up. Regularly reviewing these metrics will help you identify trends, patterns, and areas of concern.

3. **Identify strengths and weaknesses**: Compare your KPIs against your benchmarks to identify areas where you are performing well and areas that need improvement. Focus on leveraging your strengths and addressing weaknesses to optimize your campaigns.

4. **Experiment and test**: Use A/B testing and other experimentation techniques to test different strategies and tactics. By comparing the performance of different variations, you can identify the most effective approaches and refine your campaigns accordingly.

5. **Optimize and refine**: Based on the insights gained from analyzing your KPIs, make data-driven decisions to optimize your campaigns. This may involve

adjusting your targeting, refining your messaging, or improving the user experience on your website.

6. **Continuously improve**: Affiliate marketing is an ongoing process, and it requires continuous learning and improvement. Stay up-to-date with industry trends, explore new strategies, and adapt to changes in the market to maintain long-term success.

By analyzing your KPIs and making data-driven decisions, you can optimize your affiliate marketing campaigns, increase your conversion rates, and ultimately work towards earning a six-figure income per month. Remember, success in affiliate marketing requires patience, persistence, and a willingness to adapt and improve based on the insights gained from analyzing your KPIs.

10.3 Optimizing Conversion Rates

Once you have set up your affiliate marketing business and started driving traffic to your website, the next step is to optimize your conversion rates. Conversion rate optimization (CRO) is the process of improving the percentage of visitors who take a desired action on your website, such as making a purchase or signing up for a newsletter. By optimizing your conversion rates, you can maximize your affiliate sales and increase your overall revenue. In this section, we will explore some strategies and techniques to help you optimize your conversion rates and achieve your income goals.

Understanding Conversion Rate Optimization

Conversion rate optimization is all about improving the effectiveness of your website and marketing efforts to generate more conversions. A conversion can be any desired action that you want your visitors to take, such as making a purchase, filling out a form, or subscribing to your email list. By optimizing your conversion rates, you can increase the number of visitors who take these desired actions, ultimately leading to more sales and higher revenue.

To effectively optimize your conversion rates, it's important to understand your target audience and their behavior on your website. By analyzing data and metrics, you can identify areas of improvement and implement strategies to enhance the user experience and encourage more conversions.

Conducting A/B Testing

A/B testing, also known as split testing, is a powerful technique to optimize your conversion rates. It involves creating two or more versions of a webpage or marketing element and testing them against each other to determine which one performs better. By comparing different variations, you can identify the elements that have the most impact on your conversion rates and make data-driven decisions to improve your results.

When conducting A/B tests, it's important to focus on one element at a time. For example, you can test different headlines, call-to-action buttons, or color schemes. By isolating variables, you can accurately measure the impact of each change on your conversion rates. It's also crucial to have a large enough sample size to ensure statistical significance.

Optimizing Landing Pages

Landing pages play a crucial role in converting visitors into customers. A well-designed and optimized landing page can significantly improve your conversion rates. Here are some tips to optimize your landing pages:

1. Clear and Compelling Headline: Your headline should grab the attention of your visitors and clearly communicate the value proposition of your offer. It should be concise, persuasive, and aligned with the expectations set by your marketing campaigns.

2. Engaging and Relevant Content: The content on your landing page should be informative, engaging, and relevant to your target audience. Use persuasive copywriting techniques to highlight the benefits of your product or service and address any objections or concerns your visitors may have.

3. Strong Call-to-Action (CTA): Your call-to-action should be clear, prominent, and compelling. Use action-oriented language and create a sense of urgency to encourage visitors to take the desired action. Test different variations of your CTA to find the most effective one.

4. Simple and Intuitive Design: Keep your landing page design clean, uncluttered, and easy to navigate. Use visual elements strategically to draw attention to important information and guide visitors towards your call-to-action.

5. Mobile Optimization: With the increasing use of mobile devices, it's crucial to ensure that your landing pages are mobile-friendly. Optimize your design and layout for smaller screens, and make sure your forms and buttons are easy to use on mobile devices.

Improving Website Speed and Performance

Website speed and performance have a significant impact on user experience and conversion rates. Slow-loading websites can frustrate visitors and lead to high bounce rates. Here are some strategies to improve your website speed and performance:

1. Optimize Images: Compress and optimize images to reduce file sizes without compromising quality. Use image formats that are suitable for the web, such as JPEG or PNG.

2. Minify CSS and JavaScript: Minify your CSS and JavaScript files to remove unnecessary characters and reduce file sizes. This can help improve page load times.

3. Enable Browser Caching: Enable browser caching to store static files on visitors' devices, reducing the need to download them with each visit. This can significantly improve page load times for returning visitors.

4. Use Content Delivery Networks (CDNs): CDNs distribute your website's content across multiple servers worldwide, reducing the distance between your website and your visitors. This can help improve page load times, especially for visitors located far from your server.

5. Regularly Update and Maintain Your Website: Keep your website's software, plugins, and themes up to date to ensure optimal performance and security. Regularly monitor your website for any issues or errors that may affect user experience.

Implementing Trust Signals

Trust signals are elements on your website that build trust and credibility with your visitors. By instilling confidence in your brand and products, trust signals can help increase your conversion rates. Here are some trust signals you can implement:

1. Customer Reviews and Testimonials: Display positive reviews and testimonials from satisfied customers to showcase social proof and build trust.

2. Trust Badges and Certifications: Display trust badges, security seals, and certifications to assure visitors that their personal information is safe and secure.

3. Clear Privacy Policy and Terms of Service: Clearly communicate your privacy policy and terms of service to establish transparency and build trust.

4. Contact Information: Provide clear and easily accessible contact information, including a phone number, email address, and physical address. This helps visitors feel more confident in doing business with you.

5. Money-Back Guarantee: Offer a money-back guarantee to reduce the perceived risk for potential customers. This can help alleviate any concerns they may have about purchasing your products or services.

Analyzing and Monitoring Data

To effectively optimize your conversion rates, it's important to analyze and monitor data regularly. Use web analytics tools, such as Google Analytics, to track key performance indicators (KPIs) and identify areas for improvement. Some important metrics to monitor include:

1. Conversion Rate: Measure the percentage of visitors who take the desired action on your website, such as making a purchase or signing up for a newsletter.

2. Bounce Rate: Monitor the percentage of visitors who leave your website without taking any action. A high bounce rate may indicate issues with your landing pages or user experience.

3. Average Session Duration: Track how long visitors spend on your website. Longer session durations may indicate higher engagement and interest in your content.

4. Exit Pages: Identify the pages where visitors are most likely to leave your website. Optimize these pages to encourage visitors to stay longer and take the desired action.

By regularly analyzing and monitoring data, you can identify trends, patterns, and areas for improvement. Use this information to make data-driven decisions and continuously optimize your conversion rates.

In conclusion, optimizing conversion rates is a crucial step in maximizing your affiliate marketing income. By implementing strategies such as A/B testing, optimizing landing pages, improving website speed and performance, implementing trust signals, and analyzing data, you can increase your conversion rates and achieve your income goals. Remember to continuously monitor and tweak your strategies to stay ahead of the competition and maintain long-term success in affiliate marketing.

10.4 Testing and Tweaking Affiliate Strategies

Once you have set up your affiliate marketing business and implemented various strategies to drive traffic and generate sales, it is crucial to continuously test and tweak your affiliate strategies to maximize your income potential. Testing and tweaking involve experimenting with different approaches, analyzing the results, and making adjustments based on the data you gather. In this section, we will explore the importance of testing and tweaking your affiliate strategies and provide you with practical tips to optimize your performance.

The Importance of Testing and Tweaking

Testing and tweaking your affiliate strategies is essential for several reasons. Firstly, it allows you to identify what works and what doesn't. By testing different approaches, you can determine which strategies are most effective in driving traffic, generating leads, and converting sales. This knowledge enables you to focus your efforts on the strategies that yield the best results, saving you time and resources.

Secondly, testing and tweaking help you stay ahead of the competition. The affiliate marketing landscape is constantly evolving, and what works today may not work tomorrow. By continuously testing and tweaking your strategies, you can adapt to changes in the market and stay ahead of your competitors. This proactive approach ensures that you are always optimizing your performance and maximizing your income potential.

Lastly, testing and tweaking allow you to uncover hidden opportunities. Sometimes, small adjustments to your strategies can lead to significant improvements in your results. By analyzing the data and making incremental changes, you may discover new avenues for growth and uncover untapped potential within your affiliate marketing business.

Practical Tips for Testing and Tweaking

To effectively test and tweak your affiliate strategies, consider implementing the following practical tips:

1. Set Clear Goals and Metrics

Before you begin testing, it is crucial to define clear goals and metrics to measure your performance. Determine what specific outcomes you want to achieve, such as increasing click-through rates, improving conversion rates, or boosting average order value. By setting clear goals and metrics, you can track your progress and measure the impact of your testing efforts accurately.

2. Conduct A/B Testing

A/B testing, also known as split testing, involves comparing two versions of a webpage, email, or advertisement to determine which one performs better. For example, you can create two different landing pages and direct equal amounts of traffic to each. By analyzing the conversion rates of each page, you can identify which version is more effective and make data-driven decisions to optimize your strategies.

3. Test Different Traffic Sources

Experiment with different traffic sources to diversify your affiliate marketing efforts. Test various platforms such as search engines, social media networks, email marketing, and content marketing. By testing different traffic sources, you can identify which platforms drive the most targeted and high-converting traffic to your website.

4. Analyze User Behavior

Use analytics tools to gain insights into user behavior on your website. Analyze metrics such as bounce rate, time on site, and conversion funnels to understand how visitors interact with your content and offers. This data can help you identify areas for improvement and optimize your website's user experience to increase conversions.

5. Test Different Affiliate Programs and Products

Not all affiliate programs and products are created equal. Test different affiliate programs and products within your niche to find the ones that resonate best with your audience. Look for programs and products that offer high commissions, have a good reputation, and align with your target audience's needs and interests.

6. Monitor and Track Key Performance Indicators (KPIs)

Regularly monitor and track key performance indicators (KPIs) to assess the effectiveness of your affiliate strategies. Some essential KPIs to track include click-through rates, conversion rates, average order value, and return on investment (ROI). By analyzing these metrics, you can identify areas that need improvement and make data-driven decisions to optimize your performance.

7. Implement Changes Incrementally

When making adjustments based on your testing results, it is essential to implement changes incrementally. Making too many changes at once can make it challenging to determine which specific adjustment led to the improvement or decline in performance. By implementing changes incrementally, you can isolate the impact of each adjustment and make more informed decisions.

8. Stay Up-to-Date with Industry Trends

The affiliate marketing industry is constantly evolving, with new trends and strategies emerging regularly. Stay up-to-date with industry news, attend conferences, and join relevant communities to stay informed about the latest developments. By staying current, you can identify new opportunities and adjust your strategies accordingly.

9. Learn from Your Competitors

Monitor your competitors' affiliate marketing strategies and learn from their successes and failures. Analyze their websites, content, and promotional tactics to gain insights into what works in your niche. While it is essential to differentiate yourself from your competitors, understanding their strategies can provide valuable insights and inspiration for your own testing and tweaking efforts.

10. Keep Testing and Tweaking

Testing and tweaking should be an ongoing process in your affiliate marketing business. Continuously test new ideas, analyze the results, and make adjustments based on the data you gather. By adopting a mindset of continuous improvement, you can optimize your affiliate strategies and unlock your full income potential.

Remember, testing and tweaking your affiliate strategies is not a one-time task but an ongoing process. By continuously experimenting, analyzing data, and making informed adjustments, you can optimize your performance, increase your income, and achieve long-term success in affiliate marketing.

Maintaining Long-Term Success in Affiliate Marketing

11.1 Staying Up-to-Date with Industry Trends

To maintain long-term success in affiliate marketing and continue earning a six-figure income per month, it is crucial to stay up-to-date with industry trends. The affiliate marketing landscape is constantly evolving, and staying ahead of the curve can give you a competitive edge and ensure your strategies remain effective. In this section, we will explore some key strategies to help you stay informed and adapt to the ever-changing affiliate marketing industry.

1. Follow Industry Blogs and News Websites

One of the best ways to stay updated with industry trends is by following reputable affiliate marketing blogs and news websites. These platforms often provide valuable insights, tips, and news about the latest developments in the industry. Some popular affiliate marketing blogs include Affiliate Summit, Affiliate Marketing Blog, and Charles Ngo's Blog. Additionally, websites like Affiliate Marketing News and Affiliate Marketing Insider regularly publish news and updates related to the industry.

By regularly reading these blogs and news websites, you can stay informed about new affiliate programs, emerging niches, changes in advertising policies, and other important industry updates. This knowledge will help you make informed decisions and adjust your strategies accordingly.

2. Attend Affiliate Marketing Conferences and Events

Attending affiliate marketing conferences and events is another excellent way to stay up-to-date with industry trends. These events bring together industry experts, affiliate marketers, and affiliate networks, providing a platform to learn from the best and network with like-minded individuals.

Conferences like Affiliate Summit, Affiliate World Europe, and Traffic & Conversion Summit offer valuable insights through keynote speeches, panel discussions, and workshops. You can learn about the latest strategies, emerging trends, and network with industry leaders. Additionally, these events often have exhibition halls where you can connect with affiliate networks and explore new opportunities.

3. Join Affiliate Marketing Forums and Communities

Participating in affiliate marketing forums and communities is a great way to stay connected with other affiliate marketers and learn from their experiences. Platforms like Warrior Forum, AffiliateFix, and Stack That Money have active communities where members share insights, ask questions, and discuss industry trends.

By actively engaging in these forums, you can gain valuable knowledge, exchange ideas, and stay updated with the latest trends. Additionally, you can build relationships with other affiliate marketers, which can lead to collaborations and partnerships in the future.

Social media platforms like Twitter, LinkedIn, and Facebook can be valuable sources of industry information. Many influential affiliate marketers share their insights, strategies, and updates on these platforms. By following them, you can gain valuable knowledge and stay updated with the latest trends.

Some well-known affiliate marketers to follow on social media include Neil Patel, Pat Flynn, Charles Ngo, and John Chow. They regularly share valuable content, industry news, and updates that can help you stay ahead in the affiliate marketing game.

Another effective way to stay up-to-date with industry trends is by subscribing to industry newsletters and podcasts. Many affiliate marketing experts and companies have newsletters that provide valuable insights, case studies, and updates.

Podcasts like "The Affiliate Guy Daily" by Matt McWilliams, "The Smart Passive Income Online Business and Blogging Podcast" by Pat Flynn, and "The Authority Hacker Podcast" by Gael Breton and Mark Webster offer valuable information and interviews with industry experts.

By subscribing to these newsletters and podcasts, you can receive regular updates directly in your inbox or listen to them on the go, ensuring you never miss out on important industry trends.

Monitoring affiliate marketing forums and Q&A platforms like Quora and Reddit can provide valuable insights into the challenges and trends in the industry. These platforms often have discussions related to affiliate marketing, where industry experts and experienced marketers share their knowledge and experiences.

By actively participating in these discussions or simply observing them, you can gain insights into the latest trends, challenges, and strategies that are working for others. This information can help you adapt your own strategies and stay ahead of the competition.

Monitoring your competitors and industry leaders can provide valuable insights into the latest trends and strategies that are working well. Follow their websites, social media profiles, and newsletters to stay updated with their activities and learn from their successes.

By analyzing their strategies, content, and promotions, you can identify emerging trends and incorporate them into your own affiliate marketing efforts. However, it is important to maintain your unique approach and not simply copy what others are doing.

8. Continuously Educate Yourself

Lastly, to stay up-to-date with industry trends, it is essential to continuously educate yourself. The affiliate marketing industry is dynamic, and what works today may not work tomorrow. By investing in your knowledge and skills, you can adapt to changes and stay ahead of the competition.

Read books, take online courses, attend webinars, and participate in workshops to enhance your understanding of affiliate marketing. Platforms like Udemy, Coursera, and Skillshare offer a wide range of courses on affiliate marketing and related topics.

Remember, staying up-to-date with industry trends is not a one-time task but an ongoing process. By consistently following these strategies and actively seeking knowledge, you can maintain long-term success in affiliate marketing and continue earning a six-figure income per month.

11.2 Continuously Learning and Improving

To achieve long-term success in affiliate marketing and earn a six-figure income per month, it is crucial to continuously learn and improve your skills and strategies. The affiliate marketing industry is constantly evolving, and staying ahead of the curve is essential to maintain a competitive edge. In this section, we will explore the importance of continuous learning and improvement in affiliate marketing and provide practical tips to help you stay on top of your game.

The Importance of Continuous Learning

Affiliate marketing is a dynamic field that requires you to adapt to changing trends, technologies, and consumer behaviors. By continuously learning and improving, you can:

1. Stay Updated with Industry Trends: The digital marketing landscape is constantly evolving, and new trends emerge regularly. By staying updated, you can identify new opportunities, leverage emerging platforms, and adjust your strategies accordingly.

2. Enhance Your Skills: Continuous learning allows you to enhance your skills and knowledge in various areas of affiliate marketing, such as SEO, content creation, social media marketing, and conversion optimization. This enables you to become a well-rounded marketer and deliver better results.

3. Keep Up with Algorithm Changes: Search engines and social media platforms frequently update their algorithms, which can significantly impact your affiliate marketing efforts. By staying informed about these changes, you can adapt your strategies to maintain visibility and drive targeted traffic to your website.

4. Discover New Affiliate Programs and Products: The affiliate marketing landscape is vast, and new programs and products are constantly being introduced. By continuously learning, you can discover new opportunities to promote high-converting products and earn higher commissions.

Strategies for Continuous Learning and Improvement

Now that we understand the importance of continuous learning, let's explore some strategies to help you stay ahead in the affiliate marketing game:

1. Follow Industry Experts and Influencers

One of the best ways to stay updated with industry trends and learn from the best is by following industry experts and influencers. Subscribe to their blogs, podcasts, and YouTube channels, and follow them on social media platforms. Engage with their content, ask questions, and learn from their experiences and insights. Some notable affiliate marketing experts include Neil Patel, Pat Flynn, and John Chow.

2. Join Affiliate Marketing Forums and Communities

Affiliate marketing forums and communities provide a platform for marketers to connect, share knowledge, and learn from each other. Participate in discussions, ask questions, and contribute your expertise. Some popular forums and communities include Warrior Forum, AffiliateFix, and StackThatMoney.

3. Attend Affiliate Marketing Conferences and Events

Attending affiliate marketing conferences and events is an excellent way to network with industry professionals, learn from expert speakers, and stay updated with the latest trends. Some notable conferences include Affiliate Summit, Traffic & Conversion Summit, and Affiliate World Europe.

4. Invest in Affiliate Marketing Courses and Training

There are numerous online courses and training programs available that can help you enhance your affiliate marketing skills. Look for reputable courses taught by industry experts and invest in those that align with your learning goals. Some popular platforms for online courses include Udemy, Coursera, and ClickBank.

5. Experiment and Test New Strategies

Continuous learning also involves experimenting with new strategies and testing their effectiveness. Keep an open mind and be willing to try new approaches to see what works best for your niche and target audience. Split testing, also known as A/B testing, can help you compare different variations of your marketing campaigns and identify the most effective ones.

6. Analyze and Learn from Data

Data analysis is a crucial aspect of continuous improvement in affiliate marketing. Regularly analyze your key performance indicators (KPIs) such as conversion rates, click-through rates, and revenue generated. Identify patterns, trends, and areas for improvement. Use analytics tools like Google Analytics and affiliate network reports to gain insights into your performance.

7. Network with Other Affiliate Marketers

Networking with other affiliate marketers can provide valuable insights, collaboration opportunities, and support. Join online communities, attend meetups, and connect with like-minded individuals. By sharing experiences and learning from each other, you can accelerate your growth and success in affiliate marketing.

Conclusion

Continuous learning and improvement are essential for long-term success in affiliate marketing. By staying updated with industry trends, enhancing your skills, and adapting to changes, you can maintain a competitive edge and increase your chances of earning a six-figure income per month. Follow industry experts, join forums, attend conferences, invest in courses, experiment with new strategies, analyze data, and network with other affiliate marketers. Remember, the affiliate marketing landscape is ever-evolving, and those who continuously learn and improve are the ones who thrive.

11.3 Building a Brand and Reputation

Building a brand and reputation is crucial for long-term success in affiliate marketing. While it may not directly generate immediate income, it plays a significant role in establishing trust, credibility, and loyalty among your target audience. By investing time and effort into building a strong brand and reputation, you can attract more customers, increase conversions, and ultimately earn a six-figure income per month. In this section, we will explore the key strategies and tactics you can implement to build a brand and reputation that will set you apart from your competitors.

Establishing Your Brand Identity

To build a successful brand, you need to establish a clear and consistent brand identity. Your brand identity encompasses your brand name, logo, tagline, colors, typography, and overall visual style. It should reflect your values, mission, and the unique selling proposition of your affiliate business.

1. **Define Your Target Audience:** Before you can establish your brand identity, you need to have a deep understanding of your target audience. Conduct

market research to identify their needs, preferences, and pain points. This will help you tailor your brand messaging and visual elements to resonate with your audience.

2. **Craft Your Brand Story:** Your brand story is the narrative that communicates who you are, what you stand for, and why your audience should choose you. It should be authentic, compelling, and relatable. Use your brand story to connect with your audience on an emotional level and differentiate yourself from competitors.

3. **Design Your Visual Identity:** Create a visually appealing and cohesive brand identity that aligns with your target audience and brand story. This includes designing a professional logo, selecting appropriate colors and typography, and creating a consistent visual style across all your marketing materials.

Building Trust and Credibility

Trust and credibility are essential for attracting and retaining customers in affiliate marketing. When people trust your brand and perceive you as an authority in your niche, they are more likely to purchase products or services through your affiliate links. Here are some strategies to build trust and credibility:

1. **Provide Valuable and Reliable Content:** Consistently produce high-quality content that educates, informs, and solves problems for your audience. This can be in the form of blog posts, videos, podcasts, or social media content. Position yourself as a trusted source of information in your niche.

2. **Be Transparent and Authentic:** Be honest and transparent with your audience. Disclose your affiliate relationships and clearly communicate the benefits and limitations of the products or services you promote. Authenticity builds trust and fosters long-term relationships with your audience.

3. **Leverage Social Proof:** Social proof is a powerful tool for building trust. Encourage satisfied customers to leave reviews and testimonials about the products or services you promote. Display these testimonials on your website and social media platforms to showcase the positive experiences of others.

4. **Engage with Your Audience:** Actively engage with your audience through comments, emails, and social media interactions. Respond to their questions, concerns, and feedback promptly and genuinely. This demonstrates your commitment to customer satisfaction and builds trust.

Establishing Thought Leadership

Establishing yourself as a thought leader in your niche can significantly enhance your brand reputation and attract a loyal following. When people perceive you as an expert, they are more likely to trust your recommendations and become loyal customers. Here are some strategies to establish thought leadership:

1. **Create In-Depth and Insightful Content:** Go beyond surface-level content and provide in-depth analysis, expert opinions, and unique insights in your niche. This can be in the form of comprehensive guides, case studies, whitepapers, or industry reports. Position yourself as a go-to resource for valuable information.

2. **Guest Blogging and Speaking Engagements:** Contribute guest posts to reputable blogs and publications in your niche. This exposes your brand to a wider audience and establishes your expertise. Additionally, seek opportunities to speak at industry conferences, webinars, or podcasts to further establish your thought leadership.

3. **Collaborate with Influencers:** Collaborating with influencers in your niche can help you tap into their existing audience and gain credibility. Partner with influencers for joint content creation, co-host webinars or podcasts, or participate in interviews. This can expand your reach and enhance your reputation.

Building a Community

Building a community around your brand is an effective way to foster loyalty, engagement, and advocacy. When you have an active and engaged community, they become your brand ambassadors, spreading the word about your affiliate products or services. Here are some strategies to build a community:

1. **Create a Branded Online Community:** Establish an online community where your audience can connect, share ideas, ask questions, and provide support. This can be in the form of a forum, Facebook group, or Slack channel. Actively participate in the community and foster a sense of belonging.

2. **Organize Events and Webinars:** Host live events, webinars, or workshops where your audience can interact with you and each other. This creates a sense of exclusivity and strengthens the bond between your brand and your community members.

3. **Encourage User-Generated Content:** Encourage your community members to create and share content related to your brand or niche. This can be in the form of testimonials, reviews, case studies, or user-generated videos. Highlight and reward exceptional user-generated content to motivate others to participate.

4. **Offer Exclusive Benefits:** Provide exclusive benefits or rewards to your community members, such as early access to new products, special discounts, or personalized support. This makes them feel valued and appreciated, fostering loyalty and advocacy.

By implementing these strategies and consistently delivering value to your audience, you can build a strong brand and reputation in the affiliate marketing industry. Remember, building a brand and reputation takes time and effort, but the long-term benefits are well worth it.

11.4 Diversifying Income Streams

Diversifying your income streams is a crucial step in achieving long-term success in affiliate marketing. By expanding your revenue sources, you can reduce the risk of relying solely on one affiliate program or niche. In this section, we will explore various strategies to diversify your income streams and maximize your earning potential.

1. Explore Multiple Affiliate Programs

One effective way to diversify your income streams is by joining multiple affiliate programs. Instead of relying on a single program, consider partnering with several reputable companies that offer products or services relevant to your niche. This approach allows you to tap into different customer bases and benefit from a wider range of commission structures.

When selecting affiliate programs, focus on those that align with your target audience's needs and preferences. Look for programs that offer competitive commission rates, reliable tracking systems, and comprehensive support for affiliates. By diversifying your affiliate partnerships, you can increase your chances of earning a substantial income.

2. Create and Sell Your Own Products

Another way to diversify your income streams is by creating and selling your own products. This approach allows you to leverage your expertise and build a brand around your niche. By developing your own products, you can earn higher profit margins and have more control over your business.

Consider creating digital products such as e-books, online courses, or software tools that cater to your audience's needs. These products can be sold directly through your website or through popular platforms like ClickBank or JVZoo. By offering your own products, you can establish yourself as an authority in your niche and generate additional revenue streams.

3. Offer Consulting or Coaching Services

If you have extensive knowledge and experience in your niche, consider offering consulting or coaching services. Many people are willing to pay for personalized guidance and advice to achieve their goals. By leveraging your expertise, you can provide one-on-one or group coaching sessions, helping your clients achieve success in their endeavors.

To offer consulting or coaching services, create a dedicated page on your website outlining your services, pricing, and testimonials from satisfied clients. Promote your services through your content, email marketing campaigns, and social media channels. By diversifying your income with consulting or coaching services, you can generate additional revenue while helping others succeed.

4. Monetize Your Website with Display Advertising

If your website attracts a significant amount of traffic, you can monetize it by displaying advertisements. Programs like Google AdSense allow you to earn money by placing relevant ads on your website. When visitors click on these ads, you earn a portion of the advertising revenue.

To maximize your earnings from display advertising, focus on optimizing your website's design and user experience. Ensure that the ads are strategically placed without overwhelming your content. Additionally, consider using ad networks that offer higher payouts or negotiate direct advertising deals with relevant companies in your niche.

5. Explore Sponsored Content and Influencer Marketing

As your website gains traction and your audience grows, you can explore sponsored content and influencer marketing opportunities. Many companies are willing to pay for sponsored blog posts, social media mentions, or product reviews to reach your audience. By partnering with relevant brands, you can earn additional income while providing valuable content to your audience.

When engaging in sponsored content or influencer marketing, it's essential to maintain transparency and authenticity. Only promote products or services that align with your values and genuinely benefit your audience. By building trust with your audience, you can create long-term partnerships and generate consistent income through sponsored collaborations.

6. Explore Joint Ventures and Partnerships

Collaborating with other affiliate marketers or businesses in your niche can also diversify your income streams. Joint ventures and partnerships allow you to leverage each other's strengths and expand your reach. By combining resources and expertise, you can create mutually beneficial opportunities for growth and increased revenue.

Consider reaching out to other affiliate marketers or businesses in your niche to explore potential collaborations. This could involve co-creating products, hosting joint webinars or events, or cross-promoting each other's content. By working together, you can tap into new audiences and generate additional income through shared efforts.

7. Invest in Other Income-Generating Assets

Finally, consider diversifying your income streams by investing in other income-generating assets. This could include real estate, stocks, bonds, or other businesses. By diversifying your investments, you can create passive income streams that supplement your affiliate marketing earnings.

Before investing, conduct thorough research and seek professional advice to ensure you make informed decisions. Diversifying your income through investments can provide stability and long-term financial growth, reducing your reliance on affiliate marketing alone.

In conclusion, diversifying your income streams is essential for long-term success in affiliate marketing. By exploring multiple affiliate programs, creating your own products, offering consulting services, monetizing your website with display advertising, exploring sponsored content and influencer marketing, engaging in joint ventures and partnerships, and investing in other income-generating assets, you can maximize your earning potential and reduce the risk of relying solely on one source of income. Embrace these strategies and adapt them to your unique circumstances to create a sustainable and profitable affiliate marketing business.